THE WILD ADVANTAGE

What People Are Saying About *The Wild Advantage*

"*The Wild Advantage* is a powerful reminder that nature is not a distraction from innovation—it's a catalyst for it. If you want to unlock better thinking, deeper focus, and more courageous leadership, read this book, then step outside."

— Ron Schneidermann,
Former CEO of AllTrails

"*The Wild Advantage* is a must-read. Crazy creativity and next-level productivity? It's waiting outside—and Jessica hands you the key with humor, heart, and zero BS. This book is funny, fearless, and gets you outside where the magic happens. Read it—and get moving."

— Mike Pawlawski,
World Champion Quarterback,
Bestselling Author of *Every Day Great*, and Host of *Gridiron Outdoors*

"Who knows the next game-changing strategy for your business? Not a consultant. Not ChatGPT. Not your mentor, your boss, or your board. Jessica reminds you that *you* do. It's incubating in your mind. She shows you how to reveal it. Read *The Wild Advantage* and then . . . go outside."

— Monica Rothgery,
Former COO of KFC, US, and Bestselling Author of *Lessons from the Drive-Thru*

"Jess is a business shaman in hiking boots—seriously. This isn't a woo-woo exaggeration. She understands business at the cellular level and has a rare ability to cut through our own noise, leading us to something completely real. The method in this book creates space for magic to happen. It will change how you lead, how you recover, how you energize, and how you relate. Getting outside and unplugging is the reset we didn't know we needed. Very unique book. Required reading."

— Tom Roberts,
Principal and Founder of Cranberry Leadership International

"*The Wild Advantage* exposes how our screen-saturated, always-on world is rewiring our brains, draining our health, and degrading our sense of self. But Jessica doesn't stop at the diagnosis, offering a clear, actionable plan through intentional time in nature. No matter where you live, her step-by-step process helps you reclaim health, clarity, and purpose. After completing the Hike to Become Challenge, I can confidently say that this book won't just inspire you; it will change your life if you let it."

— Andrew Hartman,
Founder of Time Boss

"*The Wild Advantage* by Jessica DeAngelo is a bold, inspiring call to reconnect with nature as a path to greater creativity, clarity, and leadership. Through personal stories and backed by science, Jessica shows that unplugging from technology and stepping outside isn't just good for the soul—it's the smartest business move you can make. Fresh, witty, and actionable, this book is a must-read for anyone ready to break free from burnout and rediscover their best self."

— John Finch,
President and CEO of Legacy Group

"The Wild Advantage is a powerful reminder that when we walk in nature without distraction, we reconnect with the one person who matters most: ourselves. Jessica's roadmap to presence and awareness is simple, practical, and transformative. Follow it, and you just might find the world opening up in unimaginable ways."

— Brad Root,
Senior Vice President of Sales,
Mannington Commercial

"Before this book, my daily walks were just that—steps, noise, distraction. *The Wild Advantage* gave me the permission (and the challenge) to unplug, hike without tech, and finally *think*. Not just about work, but about how I'm showing up authentically in my life and my work. If you're craving more clarity, more connection, and a bold new way to lead—this book is your trailhead."

— Carson Green,
Vice President, Global and Enterprise Accounts,
Mohawk Group

THE WILD ADVANTAGE

Why Your Brain on Nature Is Your Boldest Business Move

JESSICA DeANGELO

Copyright © 2025, Jessica DeAngelo

All rights reserved. No part of this book may be used or reproduced by any means, graphic, electronic, or mechanical (including any information storage retrieval system) without the express written permission from the author, except in the case of brief quotations for use in articles and reviews wherein appropriate attribution of the source is made.

Publishing support provided by
Ignite Press
55 Shaw Ave. Suite 204
Clovis, CA 93612
www.IgnitePress.us

ISBN: 979-8-9994961-0-2
ISBN: 979-8-9994961-2-6 (Hardcover)
ISBN: 979-8-9994961-1-9 (E-book)

For bulk purchases and for booking, contact:

Jessica DeAngelo
jess@jessicadeangelo.com
www.jessicadeangelo.com

Because of the dynamic nature of the internet, web addresses or links contained in this book may have been changed since publication and may no longer be valid. The content of this book and all expressed opinions are those of the author and do not reflect the publisher or the publishing team. The author is solely responsible for all content included herein.

Library of Congress Control Number: 2025915533

Cover design by Graphique Design Co.
Edited by Cathy Cruise and Elizabeth Arterberry
Interior design by Jetlaunch

FIRST EDITION

For everyone stuck in a modern world, with a little bit of <u>wild</u> inside.

Trail Guide
Join the Hike to Become Challenge

This is your invitation to get outside,
get quiet, and get clear.

Scan the QR code or visit jessicadeangelo.com/trail-guide to join the challenge and access everything you need to begin, including trail-tested tips and FAQs like:

- How do I remember all the wild ideas I unlock?
- What if I don't feel safe without my phone?
- Do I make eye contact with a moose?

It's all here.

Table of Contents

Introduction: This Is Your Trailhead xv

The Great Disconnection

Chapter 1: We Have a Connection Problem. . 3
Chapter 2: Hike to Become. 18
Chapter 3: Muddy Boots are Bad for
Business. 27

The Hike to Become Challenge

Chapter 4: Hike or Walk 43
Chapter 5: In Nature: We Trust. 59
Chapter 6: Keep Tech Off. 73
Chapter 7: Every Day: For 31 Days 87
Chapter 8: Your Brain on Nature 100

The Mountain in Your Mind

Chapter 9: Becoming Fearless 121
Chapter 10: Developing Radical
Self-Awareness 137

Chapter 11: Cultivating Powerful Presence............ 152

Chapter 12: The Wild Advantage........ 167

Epilogue: There's No Wi-Fi in the Woods.. 185

Acknowledgments.................... 193

Help Me Start a Wild Movement (The Good Kind)..................... 197

Want the Author to Come Speak to Your Organization?................... 199

Sources and Inspiration............... 201

About the Author..................... 219

Introduction

This Is Your Trailhead

The journey to write this book started as an unexpected adventure. But, somewhere along the way, it stopped being about my adventure and started being about everyone I've shared the trail with, both literally and metaphorically. You picked up this book for a reason. You have a little bit of *wild* inside, but you still have to exist in a modern world. That's exactly who I wrote this book for, because I'm just like you.

I spent years in corporate America working with Fortune 100 companies, traveling the world, and creating business strategies around innovation and sustainability. But this isn't a burnout-to-passion story—it's the opposite. I want to teach you how to show up authentically in a world full of noise and give you the tools to find yourself again. While you don't have to run off into the woods to find clarity and purpose, you do have to be willing to step outside the box of an office and the paradigm of conventional thinking.

The slow creep of constant connectivity has led us into the greatest disconnection crisis humanity has ever faced. It's showing up everywhere, but nowhere is it more costly than in our work. We're trapped in a trillion-dollar attention economy where everyone wants seconds of our time while selling us solutions that ignore the one thing that matters most: ourselves.

A moment with my daughter led me to a freezing cold morning hike that changed everything. As I wrestled with finishing this book, I was torn: Is this personal development or business strategy? A no-BS conversation with my friend and bestselling author, Mike Pawlawski, reminded me it's both. You can't have one without the other. We spend so much time separating life and work, but this book is a map to help you show up authentically in both. What I discovered is that when you commit to showing up for yourself, you start showing up for everyone around you, and that's when you unlock some pretty wild ideas.

I've worked with Fortune 100 executives, founders, and entrepreneurs, and everyone is searching for the same thing: clarity. What are they trying to get clear about? Well, the same three things that led me out into nature. Who am I? What am I here on this planet to do? And how do I show up authentically as that person in my life and my work? The

INTRODUCTION: THIS IS YOUR TRAILHEAD

one place that unlocks that level of clarity is in nature. But it's a bit more nuanced than that. You don't need a three-month backpacking trip, or to go on safari or live in the woods. You just need to commit to showing up. The method in this book is shockingly simple, backed by neuroscience, and it will change the way you think about accessing the brilliance that already exists in your mind. The transformational stories in this book, both personal and professional, come from amazingly vulnerable people who chose to share their journeys to inspire you to lace up your boots and find those answers for yourself. This book will show you how to unlock wild ideas and give you a trail map to find the one person you need to meet most on the trail: yourself.

Let's get started . . .

The Great Disconnection

1

We Have a Connection Problem

Don't Look Down

At 500 feet elevation and climbing, I knew one thing: Don't look down. Actually, two things: Also, don't die. I didn't remember signing any "you might die" liability waivers, but I was in a tiny foreign country that wouldn't miss a cheeky American if she fell off the side of a cliff. I kept focusing. Two things: Don't look down and, for the love of God, don't die. I could tell by the looks on the faces of my hiking companions, I wasn't alone. We didn't expect this to be, well . . . death-defying. I think they mentioned it, but it got muffled out in my excitement. We were 2,500 feet above the Dominican rainforest, headed back up over the mountain. What seemed scary coming down felt terrifying going back up. The recent rains had made the trail more slippery than it had been on our descent, and, in some places, the trail was only about twelve inches wide, with a sheer drop off on one side. I found myself grabbing tall grass roots along the way just to create a semblance of sanity. Nobody spoke. A group of seven MBA students studying international business also decided to trust the tall grass, our internal mantras of "don't die" and some weird level of respect for the lesson nature was teaching us forging an unspoken connection. The trail conditions were forcing an evolutionary regression in our tiny brains to focus on one task . . . don't die. Every step felt more slippery than the last. But I'll tell you one thing, no one tried to snap a photograph or reach for their phone. Nature was reminding us who was boss, and for once, it wasn't the distraction of technology. The fear of dying, the exhilaration of being truly present, and the tiny moments in between made us feel human again. In our efforts not to die, we found a way to feel alive again.

> "I went into the woods because I wished to live deliberately, to front only the essential facts of life, and see if I could not learn what it had to teach, and not, when I came to die, discover that I had not lived."
>
> — Henry David Thoreau

Trapped in Boxes

The average person spends two thirds of their life "working." Not climbing mountains, not chasing dreams, not surfing waves, not exploring jungles—just working. Where do we do most of this work? Trapped inside, sitting at a desk and staring at screens. Our most brilliant ideas slip away unnoticed. The crazy part is that we've convinced ourselves this is normal. We schedule our joy into two-week vacation blocks and fantasize about a mini adventure only on the weekends. We might even be brave enough to leave the cell phone behind—for a few hours.

We live in a time that feels more connected than ever. In our modern age, we're distracted by strangers on the internet who validate our breakfast choices. We find long-lost family members through social media. We're constantly connected to coworkers through an endless stream of Slack channels that ping us at 9:00 p.m. about tomorrow's "urgent" meeting. Our phones have become like needy toddlers, constantly demanding attention with their endless notifications and alerts, providing us that addictive little dopamine hit every time we scroll.

And the irony is, humanity is struggling with the greatest disconnection crisis it's ever faced. Want to know the weather? Why open the door when your iPhone weather app can tell you? Need your morning coffee? Spend ten minutes entering your order into the Starbucks app instead of telling the barista, "Venti almond latte," and having an actual human conversation. Finally get out for that epic hike you've been promising yourself and spend most of it creating the perfect selfie instead of actually seeing the damn waterfall. We're so busy *documenting* life that we've forgotten how to actually live it.

Look at any meeting room (or Zoom screen) today. While teams discuss critical decisions about their company's future, their CEO is glued to the phone, sending a clear message that whatever's happening in their virtual world matters more than the actual humans in front of them. At home, we desperately try to maintain the illusion of work-life balance while unconsciously teaching our kids that the most important thing at any family gathering is that little black box in our hands. No wonder toddlers can find phones faster than cookies at a party—they're just mimicking what we've shown them matters most.

We're so busy *documenting* life that we've forgotten how to actually live it.

The Attention Economy

Nobel Peace Prize recipient Christian Lous Lange once said, "Technology is a useful servant, but a dangerous master." This was the same guy who helped design the blueprint for global peace that would later become the United Nations in the 1920s. He was quoted saying this almost a century before the invention of the iPhone. If anyone understood the risk of letting powerful systems run the show, it was him. Somehow he knew that in the currency of our attention, technology would replace time spent being present in our most precious relationships, even the relationship with ourselves. Olaf, the imaginary snowman in Disney's *Frozen II*, echoes similar sentiments with, "Advancing technologies will be both our savior and our doom." But here's the thing: I don't believe that technology inherently is the problem. We've just forgotten who the tool is, and our behavior reflects it.

The first time I confronted this phenomenon was in 2015, with a friend who was like a sister to me. We'd spend time together multiple times per week. Something started to change when she became more interested in her cell phone than our conversations. Lunches would involve her checking her cell phone three times before the waiter filled our water glasses. I realized that whoever was on the other end of that device was more important than me. While I eventually opted out of the friendship, it was because she left first with the currency of her attention.

The average person lives to a ripe old age of 78.4 years. It's estimated that we spend about a third of our life working, a third of our life sleeping, and a third of our life doing everything else. Time spent working equates to about 90,000 hours in an average lifespan. But what is this work we blather on about? Work can be defined as any purposeful activity that involves applying effort, skill, or expertise to produce goods, services, or results. Typically, we work in exchange for compensation. It doesn't say anything about *where* or *how* we need to work. In fact, we have only recently evolved our idea of work from outside to inside. For the entire course of human history, we essentially worked outside as hunters and gatherers. It's only been since the industrial revolution and the last few hundred years that we have moved our "work" and most of the hours of our day . . . inside. What has that done to the evolution of humanity?

While everyone is focused on the lack of connection we have with each other, the greater crisis may be our disconnection from ourselves. Ron Schneidermann, former CEO of AllTrails, has witnessed the technology-nature tension firsthand. Ron put it perfectly during our interview for this book: "I feel like we're in this existential battle versus screens. Some of the best minds in the world are spending all of their time and energy trying to keep us addicted behind screens. And that's hard. It's really a tough battle. And the single best thing I can think of to counter that is just time outside."

From someone who has built their career in the tech space and was the CEO of AllTrails, an app dedicated to getting more people outdoors, Ron's insight was revealing. While the battle we are all focused on is for the currency of our attention, the war is for our humanity.

Our Modern Life

While we build bucket lists and fantasize about dream vacations on social media, our lives are mostly spent in a nine-to-five occupation that consumes most of our waking hours, and we keep doing it trapped in the box of an office. Yet we've convinced ourselves that joy and fulfillment should somehow fit into a two-week vacation window every year. Then we wonder why we feel so uninspired in our work. The problem is we all want to be more creative, focused, productive, and connected. But the more technology is integrated into our lives and work, the less we feel capable of achieving any of it.

Let's break down a typical "modern day" on the page, because the reality of our existence is both comical and heartbreaking once you see it in black and white.

6:00 a.m. – Wake up, pee, check phone. No emergencies, just Susan's avocado toast looking delicious on TikTok. Make a mental note to try that recipe, but, like, this weekend. Because who really has the time?

8:00 a.m. – Pack lunches and wrangle family out the door. Can't leave without your phone! God forbid you're alone with your thoughts for 12 minutes.

9:00 a.m. – Back-to-back Zoom calls. Multitask like a squirrel that found old coffee grounds while mastering the art of flipping the "camera off" button. You are totally paying attention to the company forecast.

11:00 a.m. – Attempt "Deep Work Time." Your boss just initiated a last-minute all-hands meeting. Lovely.

1:00 p.m. – Notifications avalanche. Leftover lasagna in one hand, anxiety-scrolling social media in the other.

3:00 p.m. – Try for "Deep Focus" again. Instagram: "Hey, you haven't compared yourself to anyone in two hours. Now seems like an ideal distraction."

5:00 p.m. – Switch screens. Trade work emails for doom scrolling-recipes you'll never make while your kids beg for attention.

6:00 p.m. – Two choices:

1. Walk outside like an actual human.
2. Watch influencers walk outside.

You know which one you pick. There's four more hours in the day but . . . need I go on?

Now I want you to take a deep breath and ask yourself, *Am I wrong?*

The Data Doesn't Lie

And it gets better . . . or worse, really. The data on our tech addiction is terrifying. Research shows the average American checks their phone at least 344 times per day. That's once every four minutes of our waking lives. The Dscout study that tracked our relationship with little black boxes shows that the average cell phone user fondles their phone an astonishing 2,617 times daily. That's not a typo. Every swipe, tap, click, scroll equals thousands of interactions, and I'm not even talking about the time you spend cheating on your cell phone with all the other screens in your house. I'm looking at you, smart TVs and dual monitors. All in all, we spend over 11 hours consuming some form of digital media.

But one of the most sobering statistics comes from Dr. Gloria Mark's research at UC Irvine, where she's been tracking our screen-based attention for over 20 years. In 2004, people could focus on any screen for an average of 2.5 minutes before switching. Today? That's plummeted to just 47 seconds. And when we do get interrupted, it can take up to 25 minutes to fully regain focus on our original task. If you do the math, we are never fully focused. So, yes, we have a problem. Now, the question is . . . do we realize it? Apparently we do. Forty-seven percent of Americans report being "addicted to their phones," yet 74 percent of us keep our devices within reach 24 hours a day.

Like, in bed with us, or close by, or even in the bathroom. Gross. The irony is that we've created a world where we're always available, yet rarely present.

While we're all running around like chickens with our heads cut off, something bigger is happening. We're turning into workplace zombies. You know what I mean—that glazed-over look during your fourth Zoom call of the day. The one where you're "totally listening" while actually online shopping in another tab. We've mastered the art of looking busy while our brains are basically running on autopilot.

Corporate Solutions to the Wrong Problem

Then we get to the actual physical space of an office. I spent years as regional vice president of Global and Strategic Accounts for a commercial flooring manufacturer. While not reporting directly into an office myself, I spent my time traveling on behalf of Fortune 10 companies and touching down in offices all over the world. I toured office spaces and tech campuses, helping clients think about how to design the places we work to be more inviting and creative. I had a front-row seat to some of the most advanced workplaces in the world. I saw the trend of incorporating elements of biophilic design, which is a design principle that aims to create a stronger connection between humans and nature in built environments.

The problem was, it was still a box to keep humans in that we were designing. Exploring the concept for this book, I reached out to a former client, Brett Hautop, who used to be the VP of Workplace at LinkedIn. He's someone who has a reputation for pushing the cutting edge, so I wanted to hear about his newest endeavor. After leaving his former role managing global workplaces, Brett found himself ready to test more experimental forms of working. Today, he is the founding partner at Workshape, a consulting firm on a mission: radically adapting work to get the most out of getting together. During our chat, he shared with me the dirty little secret we aren't talking about in corporate America:

"Nobody ever said that this was a place they wanted to be. I keep telling developers . . . you've got a hermetically sealed box that no one really wants to be in, and, frankly, none of us grew up saying, 'Someday I want to sit in an office building underneath ceiling tiles with fluorescent lights at a plastic laminate desk. That's what I dream of.'"

We all know we don't want to be trapped in boxes. Yet we resign ourselves to doing exactly that, and we've even come up with some creative solutions to decorate our cages.

In today's age, we've got issues like "tech neck." Yeah, that's a real thing—that sexy bump forming from staring at your computer screen all day. But don't worry! Corporate America has a solution: Spend thousands on ergonomic office furniture so you never have to leave your desk. Got a standing desk? Congratulations, you've solved half the problem . . . sort of. Maybe add a treadmill under it. You can get in more calls while you exercise, because multitasking is totally working out great for us so far, right?

If we were an ancient civilization looking at ourselves, this insanity would be obvious. We're literally paying premium prices to stay trapped indoors and glued to our screens, while our most brilliant ideas slip away unnoticed. Humans have only recently become accustomed to a life lived primarily outside of nature. It wasn't until the Industrial Revolution that we moved away from a life spent outdoors. Hunting, gathering, and farming evolved into the four walls of a building, working in factories. Then, as technological advances of the 20th century brought about conveniences such as electricity and air-conditioning, we quickly became accustomed to our new home. Or, should I say "prison," trapped inside a box. In the entire history of humankind, we have never been so disconnected from the earth. Our days are spent indoors in a virtual reality. That seemed all too futuristic decades ago, but it's now become the new normal.

The scariest part? Companies know there's a problem. They see the burnout, the lack of innovation, and the void of creativity. Corporate employees, remote workers, and entrepreneurs alike are struggling to make it through another day of back-to-back meetings. The overwhelming sensation of feeling unmotivated, uninspired, and lacking what really lights us up is happening all over the world, in every company and organization, and even in our own endeavors.

But look at our solutions: We implement walking outside once a week for Wellness Wednesdays. Because we only need to be at peak performance on Wednesdays. In fact, wellness should only happen on Wednesdays because it rhymes and is good for corporate jargon. We add plants to our office space because science shows us it's good for health. Never mind that we could just walk outside and hug a tree.

Then there's the once-a-year corporate retreat, booked at a beautiful resort or location, only to pack the schedule so full that no one can actually enjoy it. Sure, there's an epic ocean view, but you'll only see it through the conference room window or during your unscheduled bathroom break. Because scheduling actual time to be in nature? That would be "unproductive."

We keep throwing money at the problem: meditation apps for the whole team, workplace wellness programs, ergonomic furniture that promises to fix everything as long as you never leave your desk, and those blue light glasses so we don't damage our eyes in our never-ending quest to be more productive.

Here's what no one's talking about: We are losing our ability to tap into our most creative, productive, and focused state because we are doing it all wrong. We say we want people to "think outside the box," but then we trap them in the box of their office, hook them up to the box of their computer, and tether them to the box of their phone. Then we're shocked when they're not having breakthrough ideas.

> **We say we want people to "think outside the box," but then we trap them in the box of their office, hook them up to the box of their computer, and tether them to the box of their phone. Then we're shocked when they're not having breakthrough ideas.**

As our companies fail us, we desperately grasp for personal solutions. We convince ourselves we need the $7,000 courses, self-help books, life gurus, or multilevel marketers posing as business or life coaches. We've forgotten that we have all the answers inside of us. We just need to create the time and environment to access them.

The Real Answer Is Free

But here's where most people get it wrong. They think the answer is some grand adventure—a three-month backpacking trip through the Himalayas or a silent retreat in Bali. While that sounds amazing (and believe me, I've fantasized about it myself), it's not a reality for most people.

We have families that need us, teams we lead, businesses we're building, companies we're running, and lives we're trying to impact. Leaving our lives to spend months in the woods, while incredibly tempting, isn't an option for most of us.

What if the answer was a little closer to home and a little more like the way we used to behave as humans? What if the answer was free? What if it can't be found through expensive consultants, wellness programs, backpacking retreats, or even a mid-life crisis? What if the answers we seek to our greatest questions have been inside of us all the whole time? All we must do is create the perfect environment for us to tap into them. What if we could discover who we truly are, why we are here, and how we can become that person in our life and work?

While my journey didn't involve climbing an epic mountain or spending months backpacking, it did involve a dose of what I've come to call *Radical Self-Awareness*, reflecting on how I wasn't showing up in my life. It was a simple moment of clarity that put it all into perspective, and that's where this story begins.

2

Hike to Become

Put Down Your Phone

One early morning in 2023, I found myself on top of a mountain, freezing my butt off as I sat in the snow and waited for the sun to come up. Several days earlier, I had reached one of those "slap you in the face" moments that only comes along when you've ignored all the other signs the universe tried to use to get your attention.

It was a Saturday, and I was at a restaurant debating what to order for breakfast, when the world's bossiest waitress told me they only had eggplant. Now, normally, I would leave this establishment, because who has eggplant for breakfast? But as the only customer in my kid's pretend restaurant, eggplant it was. And that's when my phone dinged. I looked down to answer the notification, and a few minutes later I realized that the room had gone eerily quiet for that of two toddlers playing.

As I quickly looked up to assess the damage, I was surprised to find my three-year-old daughter still standing right in front of me. With sheer disappointment on her face, she said, "Mom, put down your phone."

As I looked over at my one-year-old son, he was staring at the most important person in the room. Except it wasn't me and wasn't even my daughter. It was the little black box I held in my hands. In that moment, I was completely crushed because I realized that I wasn't being fully present in my own life. And it wasn't the first time.

If we are being honest, we've all done this and we've all had this happen to us . . . the feeling that we aren't being fully present with people we love the most. This moment was a universal wake-up call. It hit me so hard because, when I was not much older than my daughter is now, I lost my father in a tragic car accident. He didn't get the option to be present in my life. He didn't get to teach me how to swim or ride a bike. He didn't get to greet the first boyfriend that I had on the front porch, as he had always threatened to. He didn't get to give me away at my wedding and he didn't get to meet his two grandchildren. While he wasn't there for some of life's most important moments, losing my father taught me that the greatest gift we can give another human being is simply being truly present with them. We never know what day we'll wake up and it will be our last. I learned this hard lesson at four years old and that one tiny interaction with my own children brought me face-to-face with my greatest fear: that even though I was very much alive and part of their lives, I was disappearing and disconnected. But I didn't know how to fix it.

The Illusion of Work

After spending years in corporate America managing the global client portfolios of the top Fortune 100 companies and sales teams around the world, I was used to working very long hours. It was like a badge of honor, and it felt good to be a workaholic. I've always been wired that way. But I left all of that behind to pursue the path of entrepreneurship. I felt a deep pull to build my own company, establish my own mission, and be more present in my daily life with my family. In that moment, my daughter showed me I wasn't doing any of that. I was crushed. I felt like a failure as a mother and a wife. I felt like a failure as a business owner; I felt like a failure to myself. This wasn't what I thought it would be. I had left the security of a corporate paycheck, the titles, the expense accounts, the frequent flier miles, the status, and closing big deals to be more present with my family—and here I was totally *not* being present.

Entrepreneurship is a shiny object that easily deludes you into thinking it will be amazing: No more boss! Unlimited earning potential! No more useless team meetings! Making my own decisions!

Freedom and flexibility! But for anyone who has taken the entrepreneurial plunge, the reality of building your business or brand is quite different. It's exceptionally hard. If corporate America is a merry-go-round, where sometimes you just want to get off the damn ride . . . entrepreneurship is a roller coaster. Buckle up, buttercup, because the highs are higher (*I just closed a five-figure deal on my own!*) but the lows are lower (*Wait, what do you mean someone is protesting my trademark?*).

That Saturday morning with my kids, I was in the messy middle of it all: over-delivering for my clients, working myself too hard, and slowly losing the inspiration that was the kindling for starting my business in the first place. On top of it all, I was losing my ability to be present with my family. I was tired, overworked, and underpaid. But most of all, I'd lost my inspiration, my spark, my joy. And so, a few days later, with this heavy on my chest, I did what I normally do when I hit a brick wall in my life: I decided to go for a hike.

Sunrise and Epiphany

It was December 23rd—a cold morning—that I drove out to the Boise Foothills. With fresh snow on the ground and nineteen-degree temps, my car was the only one in the trailhead parking lot. I bundled up, hit the snow-covered trail, and watched my own breath as I hiked up the hill. With each step, I became acutely aware of how out of shape I was. To add insult to injury, not only was I messing up my life, failing in my business, and feeling like a terrible mother, I was also struggling to walk up a mountain. Lovely. I kept walking. I couldn't go on like this; this wasn't the "me" I knew—the person deep down inside who loved adventure, got excited by pushing the boundaries of what was possible, and sought to break the status quo. I had to find her again and, damnit, maybe she was at the top of the mountain.

I kept trekking. Finally at the top of the mountain, or rather foothill, I saw a small mound that was going to be a great place for a break, with epic views of the sun coming up over the mountain range ahead. Without common sense working, I plopped down in the snow, forgetting that my pants were definitely *not* waterproof. But I needed to sit. I was tired. I started to think about all the things I was doing wrong. I asked myself all the questions we normally do when faced with a reality we didn't mean to create: *How did I get here? What am I doing wrong?* And most importantly, *How do I fix it?*

And while nothing came to me, I slowly became aware of my butt getting uncomfortably wet. Maybe it was the cold tush, maybe it was the fresh mountain air, but something inside of me said, *Maybe you're asking the wrong questions . . . maybe what you should be asking is: When were you the happiest, the healthiest, and the most fulfilled in your life?*

As irony would have it, just as I started asking myself that question, the sun peeked over the snowcapped mountains. That's when it hit me: I've been the happiest, the healthiest, and the most fulfilled in my life when I was taking time to hike regularly. Not just on the trail, but when I was spending time in nature daily, moving my body, and unplugging from technology. Each time I'd practiced that daily habit had been after a period of disconnection with myself. But even more devastating was that the period of disconnection I'd felt often led me to make some poor life decisions. Once, when I married the wrong man, then again, when I became a workaholic during the height of the pandemic and remote working, and, finally, when I was losing my way with my family as I started out as an entrepreneur. I never gave it much thought; I just always instinctively drove to the closest park or trailhead and simply walked in nature, and then I just kept coming back, every day. Slowly, I would find my way back to myself and my life would change. So if it worked before, could it work again?

Wet Butt, Big Idea

Wet butt in the snow, I started contemplating the possibilities. Maybe I needed to go backpacking for a month, or three, and unplug to find myself again! Visions of Bill Bryson's Appalachian Trail memoir *A Walk in the Woods* and Cheryl Strayed's *Wild*—the book about her quest to find herself on the Pacific Crest Trail (PCT)—danced in my mind. I thought: *What fun! Adventure again!* But wait . . . reality snapped me back into it. I can't run off into the woods for several months. I have a family now, two tiny humans who need me, and a husband who'd worry I had been eaten by a grizzly bear . . . until he realized I left him solo with those tiny humans. Then he'd *hope* I did. I had a business I was running and clients that I had committed to. I had a community of people who depended on me. No, running off into a three-month backpacking trip was not in my future. Those days were behind me—*for now*. I wasn't a 20-year-old kid with no responsibilities anymore. So now what?

Then it hit me . . . maybe a backpacking trip wasn't what I needed. Maybe just a daily routine that forced me to get out, think, and reconnect with myself again. Maybe I could just hike daily? The competitive high achiever in me swung into full gear and I came up with a crazy idea. I decided that, since there are thirty-one days in January, I would commit to hiking for thirty-one days straight, unplugged from tech, and get back in touch with myself again. That was it. It had worked before; it could surely work again. What could possibly go wrong?

As my excitement was building, I picked myself up and started hiking back down the mountain. This was going to be epic. In fact, my revelation felt so brilliant that maybe if it worked for me as it always had in the past, I could encourage others to do it, too. I started thinking of all the positive outcomes this challenge could have; my brain was exploding with the possibilities.

One moment, I was fantasizing about my future, the next, I was starting to slip on an icy patch on the trail, feeling my foot slide out from under me. Unable to balance myself as I was falling down the hill, I ended up tumbling not once, but twice, and landed in a mound of snow and mud. Nothing quite takes you out of your excitement like a wet butt and muddy hands. That's when it occurred to me: Maybe I wasn't cut out for this. I started to let the imposter syndrome and the negative self-talk creep in. Who the hell was I to be hiking for thirty-one days straight? I was definitely not in the best shape of my life, and while I was a life-long hiker, I had recently taken a long hiatus after having two babies. Who was I to be committing to hiking daily, in January, in Idaho? I felt like a failure. I started thinking that maybe I should try painting . . . or yoga, again.

But then something magical happened. I picked myself up out of the snow and the mud and started hiking again. I acknowledged the thoughts and feelings I was having and I chose not to let them win. Because I was in nature, in movement, and not distracted by my phone or other people, I did the only thing I could think of: I started to give myself a pep talk. I realized all the reasons I told myself I shouldn't do this ridiculous self-imposed hike challenge were actually all of the reasons why I *should* do it.

Because most people are just like me. Most people can't run off into the woods and just thru-hike the

Appalachian Trail or the PCT for months to find themselves again. They have families that count on them, companies they've built, teams they lead, and a life that needs them. But behind the scenes? Most people feel some level of burnout, disconnection, and like they're operating on autopilot. Just like me, they wonder, *Is this truly it?* Is this the life they ultimately wanted to build for themselves? And, if we are being brutally honest, most people are not in the best shape of their lives.

But then an idea occurred to me:

What if we didn't have to wait to *be* the person we ultimately want to be—to *do* the things we want to do in life?

> **What if we didn't have to wait to *be* the person we ultimately want to be—to *do* the things we want to do in life?**

What if we just started showing up every day like we already *are* that person?

What if we could *Hike to Become* the person we ultimately wanted to be?

On a freezing cold trail in Boise that morning . . . an idea was born.

3

Muddy Boots are Bad for Business

How We Got Trapped Inside

Whenever I reached a point of disconnection in my life, I instinctively just drove to a trailhead to find clarity. I'm not even sure if I knew I was searching for clarity. But by getting my boots muddy, I always found it.

The very phrase "muddy boots" has become antithetical to business success. We've been conditioned to believe that high heels, a sharp blazer, beautiful offices, and shiny screens are the only acceptable markers of credibility for "real work." The idea of tracking mud into the boardroom, literally and metaphorically, feels unprofessional, messy, and disrespectful to the establishment of business.

The quiet irony is that some of history's greatest innovations and business breakthroughs didn't happen behind desks, but while walking outside. On an early morning run, Phil Knight came up with an idea: that he wanted his life to be play. This idea would inspire him to create one of the most recognizable brands in the world—Nike. Steve Jobs took some of his most important business meetings for a casual walk. Like the time he walked around Palo Alto with Greg Maffei, the former chief financial officer of Microsoft, to discuss the deal to allow integration of Microsoft's software on Apple devices. They were both in shorts and Steve was barefoot. The deal eventually went through, redefining Apple's future.

As Yvon Chouinard talks about in his book *Let My People Go Surfing*, on one of the darkest days at Patagonia, after letting go 20 percent of the workforce, he decided to take a dozen of his "top managers to Argentina, to the windswept mountains of the real Patagonia, for a walkabout." When they returned, they put together a real board of directors and started to turn the company around. The muddy boots we've been taught to avoid might be exactly what our businesses need most.

So if we are going to get our boots muddy, then we'd have to step outside—into nature. Why nature? I believe the answer lies in a brief history of our human evolution of work. Because work is where we spend most of our waking hours doing something meaningful. But the cold, hard truth is that work has evolved quite a bit in the past 150 years, which may seem like a lot of time, but it's only a speck in the timeline of human history.

First, we have the Industrial Revolution. Prior to the 1700s, it was commonplace for most people to work primarily outside: hunting, fishing, farming, and in craft trades. Then, in 1771, Richard Arkwright opened the first water-powered textile mill in Cromford, England, starting the Industrial Revolution and shifting work indoors. Enter time clocks and shift schedules. Productivity was measured in hours logged, not outcomes. Efficiency became everything. Cities were built, factories surged, and the whole of the human race started spending more time indoors than outdoors.

Nature moved from being an integral part of everyday life into something "other," only to be enjoyed during time off. As we figured out how to work in our new indoor home and shift away from our natural environment, disease surged, along with a host of human problems never seen before. However, no one seemed to ask the question, "Maybe we just don't belong indoors so much?"

After that came the office revolution. As technology got better at doing more manual things for humans, we found ourselves in more administrative roles. In 1968, another new development happened: Robert Propst's "Action Office II" system was launched by Herman Miller as the first cubicle system to effectively organize humans doing desk jobs. While it was meant to create flexibility, cubicle systems would go on to symbolize sterile indoor work. Cue *Office Space*-inspired meltdowns. Because, honestly, who wants to sit in a cubicle all day?

Later would come the open office plan revolution, and while it allowed for increased flexibility and fitting more humans comfortably in a space, it ultimately reaffirmed the idea that indoor workspaces meant people were doing actual work and had professional identity. Being inside started becoming synonymous with work and productivity, while being outside or in nature was relegated to time "off" of work, like nights, weekends, and vacations.

This was followed closely by the tech revolution that started in 1995 with the release of Microsoft Windows 95, which taught us that technology was the new identity for work. But the newfound excitement over technology masked an underlying trend taking hold. Now, you didn't just have to be inside and behind a desk or a cubicle to be considered "working." A computer screen started to creep in as yet another trait that defined productivity in the workplace. If you were behind a computer, you were obviously doing something useful.

In 2007, everything changed when Apple released the iPhone, propelling us into the digital age and redefining everything about the way we live and work. The release of the iPhone, with the integration of tech software, which appeared to allow both the freedom and flexibility to "work anywhere"—desk and office not included—replaced another unwritten societal rule. As work effectively started to escape the four walls of an office through promises of freedom, what it actually did was solidify the notion that we must always be "on."

As we are on the precipice of the great artificial intelligence revolution, we are climbing deeper into an abyss of our own making. Why step out in nature when you can use a virtual reality device to stimulate walking through a rainforest? While it is exciting to be in a world of advancing technologies, it is also silently bringing us to the brink of a huge problem: disconnection. The more "connected" we become in a virtual world, the greater the disconnection we feel from each other, from ourselves, and from our most innovative ideas.

Burnout or Bullshit?

In a world where people use "being busy" as currency and the pressure to always be "on" is suffocating, we never really stop to wonder, *What is it all for?* That is, until we reach a moment of total breakdown ourselves. Some people call it burnout. Others call it survival mode. I call it bullshit. We blame "burnout" like it's some sort of boogeyman that comes out of the office closet to steal our soul. We are the boogeymen in our own stories, but refuse to take responsibility for it. The reality is: We aren't burning out; we are choosing to light ourselves on fire. Humans are masters of deflection, and we'll keep blaming external factors while ironically looking to external factors to fix our problems.

The companies we work for are acutely aware of the situation. Wellness programs are a multitrillion-dollar industry and companies dole out their benefits like giving candy to children. Because wellness only needs to be prioritized on Wednesdays and walks in the parks are tradeoffs for eating lunch at our desk. As our companies fail us, we seek our own solutions.

> **We aren't burning out; we are choosing to light ourselves on fire.**

If you feel burnout, it's not your problem. It's your insane workload. Your boss's fault. Your company's failure to allocate resources. The demands of your clients. The stress that comes with your role.

If you feel uninspired, it's because there's no time in your day to feel inspired. You have too many deadlines, too many meetings, too many emails to sift through. If you didn't have so much responsibility, then you'd have the time to feel inspired again.

If you feel like you are sleepwalking through your own life, maybe you need to go on an antidepressant, join Orangetheory, or find a hobby that really lights you up, like clay pigeon shooting. Or maybe you should just plan that epic vacation you keep putting off.

If you feel like you're living on autopilot, maybe you should try salsa dancing, get a midlife crisis girlfriend, buy a Tesla, or quit your job to run off to South America.

The solution you dream up is never, *Maybe I should be alone with my own thoughts long enough to hear myself think?* That's too simple. Too stupid. Too easy. Too uncomfortable. Too real.

When the path ahead of us is murky, we do some crazy shit. Starting with paying lots of money to everyone for anything that might stand a chance at solving our problems.

You're Not Alone

When I first started out in my entrepreneurial journey, I wanted to live a very different life from who I was in corporate America. I knew I wanted to have a positive impact on people. I wanted to show up authentically in my work. And I knew my natural habitat definitely wasn't stuck behind a virtual screen all day.

But I really struggled to see the rest of the picture. As a business strategist whose job it is to solve this puzzle for my clients, I suddenly felt like the cobbler whose children had no shoes. Not only did

I lack answers, but I also felt shame for not being able to figure it out on my own.

So I did what we all do . . . I sought out the answers in someone else. I spent tens of thousands of dollars for coaches, consultants, brand strategists, energy healers, and website designers—literally anyone who wasn't me who could shake a stick and see into the future or my soul and tell me where I belonged.

I took course after course on some widget or marketing tactic that could solve a piece of my problem. But the real problem is . . . as we deflect, we lose the plot. Once we lose the plot, we forget what we are after in the first place.

If the problem is that we lack clarity on *who* we truly are, then of course we have no idea what we really want—or how to show up as that person in our life and work. And the idea to solve all of this at once feels really daunting. Our tiny pea-sized brains start giving up, diverting all the blood flow to our egos.

Then we become susceptible to everyone and anything that can solve a piece of that puzzle because the whole damn thing is just too much for our hyperventilating ego to handle.

$2,000 Pair of Underwear

In the early stages of entrepreneurship, I lacked clarity on all the above. But that was just too much to deal with, so I paid for an online course for someone who marketed themselves as a business coach/social media expert. I was skeptical but intrigued. She was featured in *Forbes*. You don't get featured in *Forbes* without real expertise, right? Then I took her course . . . for $2,000. I watched as she dropped her knowledge, often in flannel pajamas in bed, sipping coffee, while, occasionally, a small child would run in. She regurgitated what every Instagram influencer preaches about finding your "client avatar" and "solving just one problem," which, to anyone who has *actual* business experience, just feels like the death of integrity. That's not business. It's multi-level marketing masquerading as business strategy.

But it was the session where she talked about the importance of unsubscribing from every other email newsletter (except her own, because drug dealers prefer monogamy), cleaning out your office, and buying new underwear (I wish I was kidding) that sent me over the edge. Reality check: Did I just pay this woman $2,000 to tell me to buy new underwear?

As ridiculous as all of this might sound, the problem gets even worse in corporate America. Consultants are hired to fix a problem that: (1) they are either experts in fixing, or (2) the company just needs an outside perspective on, or both. Every year, budgets are allocated and people are spending money to get someone else to solve their greatest business challenges.

But how often do we ever step back and just give ourselves time to consider the problems we are trying to solve for the businesses we are running or the teams we are leading? Reality: almost never. Sure, we lie awake at night and we feel stress and anxiety over how to improve sales, coach up our leadership teams, or address a general lack of strategic planning. But I'm talking about walking away from it all (literally) and giving our brains a moment to breathe and contemplate the problem in real time.

In fact, the more I looked, the more I saw this problem on steroids. We are a multibillion-dollar industry built on deflecting our lack of clarity into someone else's pockets.

Humans are masters of deflection. We are so brilliant at using deflection as a survival technique to preserve our own ego that we are in denial it's even happening. Then we start to become addicted to the game—the game of finding clarity. The clarity dealers are the people who promise to solve it for us but, like any lasting addiction, the real purpose is not for them to help you find clarity but to keep you coming back for the next hit.

Now, not everyone's a drug dealer in their own game; there *are* incredible coaches, consultants, and experts out there. But the part no one wants to admit? Most people outsource the work before they've even identified or owned the problem in the first place.

Lost Without a Map

When you're deep in the wilderness, embarking on an epic hike while leading a group, there are some guiding principles that can help you. It helps if you're a strong hiker, if you've had some experience in the great outdoors, and if you have a generally good sense of direction. If you can scramble over rocks, deal with blisters in unexpected places, and be smart enough to remember to pack snacks—you're in good shape. Even if you get lost and feel the immediate panic of *Do we have enough water?* as long as you don't fall over a steep cliff or get trampled by a moose, you'll survive. You're an adventurer. But the most important part is the trail map. You have no cell coverage, but you were smart enough to pack a trail map—or download the offline version—and a trusty compass. You may get lost, but with these tools, you'll figure it out.

Now picture that same hike leader without a map. They're wandering in circles, burning daylight and energy, and rationing their last granola bar, which is really hard to do, because they are delicious.

They keep climbing switchbacks that lead to . . . nowhere. The group starts getting cranky. Doubt creeps in. Without a clear destination or a freaking map, the group loses faith in their fearless leader. Once the granola bars run out, mutiny ensues. And, eventually, they just might turn on the "leader" who led them into nowhere in the first place. Maybe they even become the snack. It's been known to happen.

Just like I experienced the illusive pull of deflection into benefiting someone else's bank account, now I sit across the table from my clients in a similar predicament. They want clarity. I want to help them find it. But I also would never pretend to be some sort of guru to give it to them. So how do I offer to help them find clarity that isn't the same thing I'm preaching against?

Quite simply: They must do most of the work. The hardest and most tactful part of my job is not to "give" anyone the answers, but to guide them into finding the answers themselves.

Muddy boots and movement may not look like the productivity we've always been taught to revere, but that's often where real clarity lives. And clarity? That's the birthplace of breakthrough ideas.

> **Yvon Chouinard** became a businessman because he would come home from climbing mountains with his head filled with ideas on how to improve each piece of clothing

and equipment he used. He created not just Patagonia, but a movement through his forward-thinking spirit, embodied in his book *Let My People Go Surfing*.

Reed Hastings reportedly dreamed up Netflix on a long walk, fuming over a $40 late fee from Blockbuster for *Apollo 13*. That stroll turned frustration into a billion-dollar disruption.

Albert Einstein famously had a breakthrough on the theory of relativity during a conversation with Michele Besso while walking home from work in Bern, Switzerland, in 1905. He even told Besso afterwards, "Thank you. I've completely solved the problem."

Nikola Tesla was strolling through Budapest's City Park, reciting poetry, when he saw the solution to alternating current. He reportedly sketched it in the dirt. Because once brilliant ideas strike, you might as well write them down.

Turns out, wild ideas don't happen when you're sitting still. They happen when you're moving, unplugged, and outside.

For me, that place has always been the trail. And research backs it up: A University of Utah study found that time spent in nature can drastically improve cognitive function and creative output by up to 50 percent.

What my intuition had known for years, science now confirms: Those muddy boots might be the most powerful business tool we've never been taught to use. Much like on the trail, the best guidance comes not from giving specific directions, but from creating the conditions where clarity can unfold and your brain can unlock wild ideas. That's what this book is here to do.

> **What my intuition had known for years, science now confirms: Those muddy boots might be the most powerful business tool we've never been taught to use.**

The Hike to Become Challenge

4

Hike or Walk

31 Days of Snow and Mud

So, back to that freezing cold foothill and me, covered in mud and snow. As my competitive nature kicked into overdrive and a commitment to hike for 31 days straight started locking into place, I excitedly drove home to tell the one person I knew would be on board: my husband. I can always count on him to push me further than I would myself. So, over morning coffee, we discussed that, while this was a crazy idea, I should give it a go. He promised that, should I slack off or not hike one day, he would hold me accountable, call it to my attention, and kick me out the front door with my boots.

So I started hiking. At first, it was novel, a welcome break from my busy routine and the demands of raising two toddlers and building a business. It was quiet time to think. It was *weird*. I wasn't used to the quiet or being alone with the thoughts in my own head. But as someone who has failed miserably at meditating and been on a backpacking trip, I knew the drill. The point is not to judge the thoughts that come into your head, but let them wash over you like ocean waves, without judgement. So I did that. Even when they were sometimes uncomfortable. I would notice them like an unwelcome rattlesnake on the trail and just keep on walking.

After about a week and half, I started to notice a few things. First, I was sleeping better. No more sleep aids or ridiculous nighttime routines. I was just tired when I went to bed. Second, my stress and anxiety were the lowest they had been in years. I also started to notice I was becoming more focused and creative in my business. My time alone on the trail allowed me to come up with crazy ideas and realize that most of what I was putting my energy toward was an avoidance of what was truly necessary to build the business. But, most importantly, I realized that, as I was learning how to be more present on the trail with myself, I was instinctively becoming what I call more *Powerfully Present* with the people around me—my children, my husband, my clients, and my friends.

Why did the Hike to Become Challenge work so well? As I started to unpack the nuances in my brain, I realized there are four critical parts to the process that I was unintentionally practicing, which had some serious science behind why it works so well. It's so easy it's ridiculous, but miss any of the four parts and it has a very diluted effect.

I love data and I love research. My friends joke that if I had a love language, it would probably be an Excel spreadsheet. So I had to know why I was experiencing all of these benefits. I wasn't surprised at the benefits I was experiencing because they had happened before, but this was the first time I was really conscious of it. I started to list out the things I was doing that were different from my normal routine. I was simply going for a daily hike. But what the hell was that? When I broke it down, I was spending time in nature, being in movement, and unplugging from technology for at least 30 minutes a day, every day. It was not novel or new. So why was it working so well? What was up with all the incredible benefits I was experiencing? Most people think that going for a hike means scaling a mountain, but it doesn't. The true definition of a hike is going for a long walk in the wilderness. I decided to reframe the word into what I was actually doing:

- H = Hike or walk
- I = In nature
- K = Keep tech off
- E = Every day for 31 days

Your Brain on Walking

The first part is H, which stands for "Hike"—or walk, for those of us averse to any outdoor activities, like my friend Stef, a staunch New Yorker who doesn't feel comfortable unless there's asphalt under her feet. To clear up any confusion, we're not talking about climbing Mount Everest here. This is about movement, and the science behind it is mind-blowing. When we walk, especially in a natural environment, our brain experiences bilateral stimulation—meaning both hemispheres are engaged and talking to each other.

In 1987, a psychologist named Dr. Francine Shapiro was taking a walk in a park when she realized that, by moving her eyes side to side, she was processing her own negative emotions at a much more rapid speed. This "walk in the park" moment was the spark that led her to invent eye movement desensitization and reprocessing (EMDR) therapy. This therapeutic method is now used to treat a wide range of issues—from processing traumatic events to PTSD and other ailments.

The basis for EMDR is creating bilateral stimulation, which helps each hemisphere in your brain communicate with the other. This results in you having increased relaxation, a greater sense of resilience, and improved executive functioning. That's your ability to think, process information, remember stuff, and make decisions. Just like Francine discovered, you also have a greater ability to process emotional distress or trauma.

To better understand what is going on in our brains when we walk, inadvertently creating bilateral stimulation, I reached out to a client, Gina Nelson,

LCSW, CDWF, a certified EMDR therapist, consultant, and trainer, as well as the owner of Authentic Gains. She told me that we try to "think" our way through problems all the time, and then hit a wall.

"Bilateral stimulation breaks down our defense mechanisms so we can't think through things," she said. "Where cognitive behavior therapy is very top-down—I'm going to think and change my thoughts and then my emotions change—EMDR is a bottom-up [approach] where we actually work through the emotions first, and when the emotions change, the thoughts change."

I asked Gina to explain EMDR in layman's terms for all of us who don't have a master's degree in psychology:

> EMDR is based off of something called the adaptive information processing model—the AIP model. What that really means is that the past is in the present. So if I'm in the present right now, and let's say my boss rolls his eyes at me and gets huffy and walks out of the room, that experience triggers something in me that's from the past experience that's happened to me. So how I respond to that is usually from a more immature part of me from a younger time. If I encode that as "I'm not important, I'm dismissed, you don't care what I have to say, my voice doesn't matter" it's most likely possible that I have had a time in my

life when my voice also didn't matter. So the past is in the present.

The problem is, we often don't ever associate the two because we never have the time and space to just think. But on the trail, without distractions, and in movement, I often find that something that was bothering me starts to melt away. I realize my reactions have more to do with my past (insecurities, fears, irrational worries) than what's really happening in the present. Instead of freaking out that someone didn't respond to an email, or a proposal didn't get accepted, I acknowledge where it's coming from (the past insecurities or unspoken fears) and realize that it's not even something to worry about in the first place. They're probably just on vacation.

What this means for you is simple yet profound: Your brain literally changes when you walk in nature. The bilateral stimulation helps the two hemispheres of your brain communicate more effectively, improving cognitive function, emotional processing, and creativity. Walking is giving your brain exactly what it needs to function better. By simply putting one foot in front of the other in a natural setting, you're activating ancient pathways that can clear mental fog, reduce anxiety, and spark innovation.

As 19th century German philosopher and father of radical ideas Friedrich Nietzsche wrote in *Twilight of the Idols*: "Only those thoughts that come by walking have any value."

He's not wrong. Stanford researchers found that walking, especially outdoors, can boost creative thinking by up to 60 percent, with benefits after the walk ends. While walking anywhere can increase creativity, it was when participants walked outdoors that the benefits included more novel and vivid ideas. I've experienced this phenomenon with my clients as well. The ideas and brain power we cultivate on the trail lasts for hours afterward in our strategy sessions.

This isn't just ancient wisdom—it's good for business. Steve Jobs was famous for his walking meetings, believing that movement stimulated creativity and problem-solving. He would regularly take important conversations outside Apple's headquarters, walking side by side with colleagues like the legendary Jony Ive, to chat about big innovations and seamless designs. It's rumored that the design of iMac G4 was agreed upon while they walked in a flower garden together. It wasn't just a quirky CEO habit either—although the whole barefoot thing is hilarious until you understand the concept of "grounding." It was a deliberate strategy that helped shape some of the most innovative products of our time. Jobs started a trend that we see in some of the most elite business minds of our time. After Jobs took a walk with Mark Zuckerberg during the early stages of Facebook (now Meta), Zuckerberg started walking more regularly to unlock business ideas. In fact, it doesn't take long to start seeing patterns between the same people who built or run business empires and those who view walking as some of their best ideation time, such as Square's Jack Dorsey, who credits walking as the best way to facilitate deep thinking.

Walking? Sounds crazy, right? We all walk, don't we? Well, here's a catch: We used to, up until the last several hundred years. The contrast between our modern sedentary lifestyle and our ancestral movement patterns is unnerving. Hunter-gatherer societies typically moved 8 to 15 miles per day, while the average American today walks less than 3,000 steps—under one-and-a-half miles. Our bodies and brains evolved for movement, yet we've practically engineered it out of our daily lives, replacing it with hours of sitting and screen time. The human body was designed to move—not to sit in front of screens for 11 hours a day, which is the average for Americans. We're literally fighting against our own evolutionary programming when we stay still for too long. While it's taxing on our bodies, it's also destroying the capabilities of our minds.

The Crazy Keynote Idea

Somewhere between freezing my ass off and mid-morning hikes, I stopped feeling uncomfortable in my own thoughts and started thinking through my greatest problem: *Why wasn't I happy or inspired in my work?* I realized I wasn't redefining anything by being a business strategist who is now consulting instead of earning a corporate paycheck. I found myself cutting-and-pasting my corporate persona into my consulting work. There was nothing novel or new in the way I approached solving business challenges and finding creative solutions.

Then I went back to reframing the question: *When was I the happiest in my work? When did I have the biggest business breakthroughs?* And, again, while on the trail sorting through my problems, the answer smacked me in the face. I kept coming back to hiking as the solution to all my problems. Then something magical happened. I started to think, *Well, this is silly. If hiking has been so impactful for me to unlock brilliant ideas, why don't I take my clients hiking?*

That's when it dawned on me. A consulting client, The Legacy Group, had recently asked me to be the keynote speaker at their company retreat at a beautiful state park outside of Seattle—The Lodge at Saint Edwards, conveniently located on miles of trails on the edge of Lake Washington in the beautiful Pacific Northwest.

Company retreats are always booked in beautiful places, but the attendees are lucky to ever see much of what's outside the hotel walls. I started to think about every other keynote presentation

I'd ever attended. After hours of being trapped in meeting rooms, subjected to death by PowerPoint, the last thing I wanted was to sit for two hours in another dark room. No matter how inspiring the speaker was, it was still hard to sit there and hear about some epic mountain-scaling adventure when we were stuck in a dark, windowless room . . . where that story *clearly* didn't happen.

So I did the only thing that seemed sensible and called John Finch, The Legacy Group's CEO and president, who hired me.

"Hey, John," I said, "I have a crazy idea—what if I broke my keynote in half, took everyone on a guided hike, and brought them back for the rest of my speech?"

He didn't even hesitate and just said, "Sure, let's do it."

Over a year later, that one "yes" had such a profound impact on me and my business that I had to ask John why he agreed right away.

"I believed in you," he said. "And I believed that your idea had weight to it, and I respect you. . . . I wanted you to be part of our organization for a lot of reasons, simply because of the energy you bring and the intentionality that you bring. So you're like, yeah, let's take them on a hike. I'm like, 'Cool. Let's do it.' There was zero hesitation."

We've worked with each other for years in one capacity or another and this man has always had tremendous faith in me. For that, I am forever grateful. Had he dismissed the idea or been hard to convince, it may have just died on the hiking trail. But as a hiker himself and someone who truly cares about his people, this man said yes when most others would have had a lot of questions.

We agreed to prepare people enough to be dressed for an outdoor walk, but not enough to tell them they were hiking mid-keynote, because part of the beauty would be catching them by surprise.

With my newfound "yes" from John, the material for my speech flowed out of me. That speech became the background for a TEDx Talk and for this book. I talked about the great disconnection problem we have, our focus on loss of connection with other people, and how, ultimately, the real disconnection is with ourselves. Fresh off my own Hike to Become Challenge, I was able to share just how transformative this experience was to get to know myself again on the trail.

I planned a hike that I felt most people could do without too much physical exertion. The morning of the keynote, I scouted it myself and realized the elevation climb back up was more than even I had bargained for. I was worried, but the front desk assured me that elderly people and children alike tackled it regularly. "Just take your time," was their advice.

When it came time during my speech, I dropped my signature line: "But do you know what's better than a picture? The real thing . . . Let's go for a hike!" The looks on people's faces were priceless—confusion, excitement, and a few "Is she serious?" glances. But all 42 of them agreed to ditch their cell phones and followed me out the door and onto the trail.

Unexpected Inspiration

While we were off to a good start on the way down, the way up was (as I feared) more of a challenge than some people anticipated. I remember one person in particular, Rick, leaning up against a tree and breathing deeply. He looked at me over his sunglasses and said, "If you take a picture of this, I'll kill you."

I didn't have my phone on me, so that wasn't a problem, and I knew him well enough to know that his death threat was a joke to mask an awkward situation: trying to hike with 42 people up a hill. We stopped frequently, and I prompted the group to share insights about their hiking buddy—a practice I still carry on today. But, honestly, it was also a clever way to buy time as we climbed our way back up the trail.

As we walked back into the conference room to finish the keynote, I noticed a shift in energy. While some individuals probably wanted to murder me on the spot for the impromptu exercise, others were revitalized. There were smiles and laughs. People were grateful to get moving. The rest of my content had way more engagement, with people leaning in because they were experiencing exactly what I'd told them about in theory—that being in nature, in movement, and unplugged would turn on their brains and make them happier humans.

The next day, I stopped at Legacy's offices before my flight home to say goodbye. As I pulled into the parking lot early in the morning, I saw Rick, the tree leaner and death threatner who had struggled on the hike. Since I'd spent time consulting with this company, I knew the employees well and I also knew I was about to get an earful. I hesitated to get out of my car, ready for criticism. Taking a deep breath, I greeted him and immediately apologized.

"I want to apologize to you for the hike I picked yesterday," I said. "It was never my intention to make you feel embarrassed."

Not one to mince words either, he shook his finger. I braced myself for a serious scolding. "I'm not gonna lie, I wasn't too happy with you yesterday," he said. "But then I realized something. As someone who spends a lot of time outdoors hunting and fishing, I just always took for granted that I'm in good shape. But what you showed me yesterday is that I'm not in the shape I think I am."

His face reddened and I could tell emotion was swelling. "I want to be in better shape; I want to be around for my grandchildren. You showed me that I have to get my ass in gear."

I was stunned. These were not the four-letter words I expected. This was never what I intended. I breathed a sigh of relief. I can't remember if I shook his hand or hugged him in that moment. I was partly relieved to not be yelled at, but the other part of me was still in awe of what he shared with me. I think I was in shock.

Over a year later, I called to ask Rick if I could put his story in the book. He was quiet on the other end of the line, and I thought, *This was a mistake. It's too raw. I'm asking too much.*

Then he said, "If you tell my story, you have to tell the rest of it."

He went on to explain to me that since that hike, he'd lost 15 pounds, was exercising regularly, and cut sugar out of his diet. The next part was what brought tears to my eyes. He told me that he had just gone out on a dirt bike excursion with his grandkids and said, "I've felt better than I have in a long time, and I didn't even get tired."

I thought back to when I wrote the speech for this group—how much I wrestled with whether or not to include losing my dad, and what that taught me as the reason behind why I do what I do—teaching people to show up and be Powerfully Present in their life and work again. Then, I realized, while it's hard for all of us to be vulnerable, the magic happens when others see themselves in your story. This was more than a hike that inspired Rick; it was a reminder of the precious time we all stand to lose when we don't show up in our own life as the happiest, healthiest, and most present person we can truly be.

This is the lesson that movement in nature teaches us. It forces us into a place of Radical Self-Awareness. John shared with me how much this experience brought to the Legacy Group's team and changed some of their everyday practices, including regular walking meetings for one-on-ones and the occasional pop-up hike before a leadership meeting.

"I know that nature works," John said. "Nature is a powerful antidote and elixir for opening people up and relaxing people to a degree where they feel they can maybe be more vulnerable . . . getting outside allows you to break down the conventional barriers that you may encounter in a typical office environment."

Often the things we are neglecting or choosing not to acknowledge come to the surface in a way that forces us to acknowledge them. The combination of nature, movement, and unplugging makes us face just how human and often fallible we truly are, but also just how much we have control over our own life and how we choose to spend it.

To start this journey, you don't need fancy hiking boots, expensive gear, or even mountains nearby. You just need to make the decision to move your body in nature. Start small—even 30 minutes a day can begin to unlock these benefits. Your brain is waiting for you to give it what it needs most—the simple rhythm of bilateral movement in the perfect environment to help you find Radical Self-Awareness and unlock a new level of clarity.

5

In Nature: We Trust

Forest Bathing: Please Keep Your Clothes On

Which brings me to the "I" in HIKE, which stands for "In nature." While we are defining things . . . "nature" is anything not made by humans. A tree-lined street, a park, a blue sky, a patch of grass—nature is all around us. So stop telling yourself you can't do it because you don't live by mountains or an epic forest.

While the benefits of being in movement create bilateral stimulation in the brain, what happens if we add in the element of being in nature? The physical and mental benefits start to exponentially increase. I wanted to know why.

As my quest for hard data began, I continued with nature. I looked up every peer-reviewed nature study I could find and read over the results. One caught my attention: It was a study on *shinrin-yoku*, known as the Japanese art of forest bathing. Now before you picture people shedding clothes and running half naked into the woods like some sort of midsummer night's dream, which inevitably happens every time I mention it in mixed company, let's unpack what it really is.

Back in the 1980s, Japan's government was seeing a health crisis. While Japanese culture is known for how much it reveres its work ethic, people were experiencing long hours, little downtime, and all the things that go along with it—the classic symptoms of burnout. But the Japanese were taking burnout to an extreme level that led to increasing cases of *karōshi*, which translates into "death by overwork." So someone had to do something.

The Japanese Ministry of Agriculture, Forestry, and Fisheries found the perfect prescription to improve well-being, reduce stress, and counteract toxic work culture—time spent in nature. Shinrin-yoku, also called forest bathing, is the simple idea of immersing oneself in nature. You go into the forest to essentially "bathe" by spending time experiencing all five of your senses in a natural environment. Imagine sitting in an old growth forest with no one around and your cell phone shut off, and simply "being."

You would take time to breathe in the crisp forest air, note the smells, and hear the sounds, such as those of small animals, birds chirping, or wind rustling through the leaves. You would look around to see a spectacular array of greens, blues, and browns that instantly calm the eye. You would feel the ground underneath you and note how you can even taste your own saliva, which you've never quite experienced before, because to be honest, you've never had the time or inclination to think about it. That is forest bathing.

As you can imagine, as it was embraced by more people, an interesting phenomena occurred; it was as if nature was the perfect prescription for burnout. People were emerging from their forest bathing experiences less stressed, more grounded, and happier. Was it all just "woo-woo" or was something more profound going on?

Finally, someone got the bright idea to study its effects. A variety of studies out of Japan in 2010 split participants into two groups: One group viewed and then walked through a forest, the other did the same in a city. The results? Wild.

The forest group saw a 13.4 percent drop in cortisol just from viewing the trees—and a 15.8 percent drop after walking through them. Their pulse rates fell by 6.0 percent just from looking at trees, and another 3.9 percent after walking through them. Even blood pressure dropped: 1.7 percent after viewing, and 1.9 percent after walking. All this, without a single breathwork session or meditation app.

The results of studies performed on the physiological effects of shinrin-yoku showed that forest environments could lower concentrations of cortisol, lower pulse rates, lower blood pressure, increase parasympathetic nerve activity (that's your "rest and digest" mode), and lower sympathetic nerve activity (that's your fight or flight mode) compared with city settings.

There's so much we have yet to uncover about the profound benefits of being in nature, but one of the most fascinating things I've read, which came from a guide called *Forest Bathing: Including Nature Therapy and Silence* by Christian Arzberger, was what substances we are breathing in when we practice forest bathing. Terpenes and fungal spores are substances that trees (and plants) emit to communicate with one another. It's like the world wide web for plants, used to communicate important information, such as warnings about diseases or even using the spores to reproduce themselves. But when we walk among these plants, especially in green areas and surrounded by trees, we are breathing in these same substances, and it has a whole host of incredible benefits for us.

In fact, by walking in a forest, you place your nose at the same height as the highest concentration of these substances for the maximum effective dose. While most people avoid being outside in the cold, rain, and fog, these are the ideal times to try forest bathing, because the concentration of these substances is heightened even more. Terpenes have been shown to have a wide range of positive effects on humans, including boosting your immune system, lowering blood pressure, supporting healing and regeneration, increasing the body's own killer T cells (that ward off diseases), and lowering inflammation levels.

> While being in nature can clearly have a positive effect on your body, it also has a tremendous benefit for your mind.

But that's not even the tip of the iceberg. While being in nature can clearly have a positive effect on your body, it also has a tremendous benefit for your mind. Just as I experienced better clarity, a reconnection to myself, and an ability to be creative, scientific studies show it doesn't take very long to start experiencing the profound benefits of being in nature. And they accumulate over time, hitting different markers the longer you stay in the woods, or desert, or park.

The 30-Minute Minimum Dose

A review of over 14 studies in the journal *Frontiers in Psychology* found that just spending ten minutes or more sitting or walking in a variety of natural settings can significantly improve both the psychological and physiological biomarkers used to measure mental well-being. What this means is that even a short duration of time spent in nature can effectively reduce stress and anxiety.

Dr. MaryCarol Hunter of the University of Michigan conducted a study to find out the minimum effective dose of nature for the greatest payoff in terms of lowering stress. "We know that spending time in nature reduces stress," she said, "but until now it was unclear how much is enough, how often to do it, or even what kind of nature experience will benefit us."

What she found was that we should spend 20 to 30 minutes sitting or walking in a natural environment to effectively lower cortisol levels. This study showed that the most efficient stress reduction occurred between 20 and 30 minutes of nature exposure, with continued but slower benefits beyond that duration.

This isn't just ancient wisdom or a well-being movement. Modern workplace researchers are proving what we instinctively know. Brett Hautop, founder of Workshape, conducted controlled experiments comparing indoor work settings with identical outdoor ones.

"We created matching settings indoors and outdoors and measured feedback," Brett explained. "We controlled light, sound, bugs—we made it so people didn't have something to use as an excuse. People consistently would say, 'I absolutely loved doing this out here' over being inside. There's undoubtedly a real truth that if you can create an environment outside, you can have an amazing experience."

Brett's workplace experiments align perfectly with what the scientific studies are reporting. When we remove the barriers and excuses, humans consistently choose the outdoor environment to do their best work.

But what I was most curious about is at what point our brains effectively "turn on," as I experienced on the trail. I didn't have to look far. Scientific studies by Dr. David Strayer and Amy McDonnell, PhD, at the University of Utah explore the idea that the 30-40 minute mark in nature seems to be the magic number to start changing the way our brains activate. What's true, but also not widely recognized, is that being in nature after the 30-minute mark or longer increases your cognitive function. Cognitive function, for those of us who skipped biology class, is our ability to think, remember information, make decisions, and use executive functioning. You know, the things we need to be operating at peak performance, but rarely have.

While everyone is focused on the well-being aspects of nature, I believe that is one of our gravest errors in human history. Obviously nature is restorative to our well-being. It is where we belong. But by focusing only on the restorative aspect of nature, we've missed the key to where it really matters—our minds. We ripped ourselves out of our natural habitat and shifted to spending most of our time on screens. Then we question why we've lost the ability to feel anything, create anything, or even solve our biggest challenges.

Humans aren't meant to be indoors most of the time. Humans didn't evolve to be stuck behind screens. Unfortunately, the studies comparing our modern-day lives to that of a hunter-gatherer society and spending our days in nature seem to be lacking. Why? Well . . . there's no money to be made in nature. Nature is free. Anyone can step outside and experience its profound benefits. But there's no product to be pushed, drug to be marketed, or expensive widget to promote. So studies on the benefits of nature are, as you may have already guessed, not well-funded. While frustrating at first, it became my resolve to write this book. What if the answers to our most pressing problems lie not in taking a drug, hiring expensive consultants, or buying fancy tech widgets? What if it really is as simple as going for a walk outside?

Our Brain on Nature

I've experienced the profound benefits of nature immersion with my clients and how it helps us do our best work. Sometimes these experiences happened quite unexpectedly.

It was pouring down rain, the kind people would say is " raining cats and dogs," and I was standing cross-armed, looking out into the parking lot of my office building with disappointment and refusing to say anything. I wasn't alone. Next to me was Dr. Zane Sterling, my newest client. We watched the rain together in a weird standoff, wondering who was going to state the obvious first. Neither one of us was afraid of getting a little wet, or hell, even muddy. But this was not the kind of VIP strategy hike I had in mind. After a few minutes, I turned to him and said, "Well . . ." and he finished my thoughts.

"Not a great day for a hike, huh?"

Nope. But we could get to work on creating a strategic plan for his newest business venture: Build a Legacy Life.

As a lifelong serial entrepreneur and a chiropractic doctor with a background in business and finance, this man had built multimillion-dollar enterprises and knew a thing or two about creating successful business ventures. But this next project was to be his legacy, which is how he came to work with me. He wanted to use his decades of business, life, and financial wisdom to teach a new generation how to become more independent and experience financial freedom. It was my job to help him take all that knowledge and build out a strategic plan, to make that a reality.

And, as with any new client, our engagement was to start with a hike, where I would ask a series of specific questions on the trail at certain times to capture honest answers. We would unpack questions that would help us find the clarity to build the business of his dreams. Imagine creating something that is both impactful *and* profitable, allowing someone to change even more lives. There was one problem: I hadn't considered that, at some point, there would be a torrential downpour. I did the only thing I knew how to do, and we went into the conference room and spent the next six hours drafting out his strategic plan.

At the end of the day, we had the start of his strategic plan and were both tired. Neither of us loved being trapped in the box of the office or on screens. As we were wrapping up, I said to him, "I'm going to make this up to you. Next week, meet me here and we'll hit the trails and finish up this plan."

He agreed. That following week, we met first thing in the morning, and the weather gods were smiling on us. It was sunny with a slight chill, perfect for a hike strategy session. We drove out to a trail that wraps around a creek, left our cell phones in the car, and started hiking.

As most of the trail was single file, I let him go first. I want my clients to see nothing but nature as they move, not even the back of my head. And by not being in front when I ask the questions, they remove me from the equation and just talk. The questions I ask are not the same ones typically explored in traditional coaching or consulting sessions, because during our time on the trail we forget about the business. I learn more about the human being behind the business. What makes them tick? What keeps them up at night? I want to know about their most memorable moments, favorite clients, worst clients, and the times they felt the most alive in building their business. I ask all sorts of questions that, for most of my clients, are the first anyone has ever asked them.

Zane shared this about his experience:

"I didn't know what to expect hiking. . . . It was very interesting to me because it didn't seem pushy or pressured at all. Ideas came through and I had answers come to me that I didn't even know were out there as you asked certain questions."

We talked about his dream to coach more people and help them build their legacy life.

"I've been thinking about this for years," he said. "You asked me a question, and it struck me, but it didn't stop me. And that was, well, 'What's taken you so long? What's holding you back? Are you afraid of something?' And that was a question I didn't necessarily expect, but that really helped me think through it. I thought, 'yeah, what am I waiting for?'"

Clients are always surprised by their own answers on the trail. I'm not; it's why I take them out on the trail in the first place. I know that being in nature, in movement, and unplugged ultimately changes the way their brains work, and the clarity they have about who they are and how to show up as that person in their work. My role isn't to have all the answers, it's to create the conditions where my clients can access their own wisdom. As Zane put it: "You were there to be a guide, and maybe open up my thoughts and pull some of those thoughts out that have been sitting dormant for a little bit."

I get to bear witness on the trail to these revelations and make sure they don't forget them. With Zane's background in movement and fitness, spending over 40 years as a chiropractor, he understood this intuitively:

"When our brains work best is when we have almost no input in terms of sound. And when are we ever without something being pushed into our brains? . . . There's a whole other dimension that opens up. When we're out on the trail, it's a different trail, if you will, and you're opened up to new thoughts . . . Instead of going down that same trail of reasoning and thought and decision-making, I was over here in another realm, going, 'Oh, this is much more creative.'"

Due to timing, and my schedule, I had to keep the hike short—just long enough to turn on our brains and create clarity. We hit the car and headed back to the office. With only an hour and half until my next client, we got straight to work. Not only did we tackle finishing his strategic plan, but we also outlined the framework for his intellectual property. What's intellectual property? It's the thing that takes people like Zane from being just a coach to a sought-after expert. It takes the form of the original ideas, creations, or lessons that only *you* can teach. In my experience, it often takes me months of working with a client to get to the place of developing an actual framework. We did it in under 90 minutes and it made sense. We developed a visual to incorporate the most useful principals he teaches his clients in an easy-to-use framework that would be the pillar of his workshop and coaching offers.

Zane noticed the difference immediately, saying, "Because we weren't using the same parameters, I was leaving some of my self-doubt and some of my thoughts behind because of the hike."

Being in movement and in nature had literally changed how his brain was processing information.

I was in awe. It's one thing to read about why being in movement and in nature works to turn on the brain. It's another to experience it, and it's a whole other universe of understanding to do it with a client and see the difference right before your eyes.

Beyond my own experience and that of my clients, I started wondering about the real business case for being in nature. This led me to dive into some of the greatest business books, searching for evidence of brilliant ideas that spontaneously emerged in natural settings. I didn't have to look far . . .

The introduction of *Shoe Dog* by Phil Knight opens with 24-year-old Phil on a run in Portland, Oregon. Recently returning home after earning an MBA from Stanford and a year-long stint in the U.S. Army, he was still unsure of what to do with his life—so he went for a run.

Knight describes that foggy morning in 1962 when his mind searched for meaning as his legs pumped faster: "But deep down I was searching for something else, something more . . . And then it happened. As my young heart began to thump, as my pink lungs expanded like the wings of a bird, as the trees turned to greenish blurs, I saw it all before me, exactly what I wanted my life to be. Play."

That morning run sparked the idea for Nike—one of the most recognizable global brands of all time. It was 1962, before cell phones or earbuds. Just a 24-year-old kid being in nature, in movement, and unplugged, spontaneously realizing he was put on this planet to *play*. He would go on to inspire millions to "Just Do It." As if you need any more inspiration to find your damn running shoes.

6

Keep Tech Off

Even Your Damn Smartwatch

Now that we've covered the first two elements of reframing what a HIKE is (H = Hike or walk; I = In nature) and all the amazing benefits to turn on your mind, there's one thing that inevitably gets in everyone's way.

The number one mistake people make when going for a walk outside? Taking the cell phone along. Do you remember the famous ad campaign from the '90s to encourage people to stop smoking? It was farm animals smoking. The tagline was "It looks just as stupid when you do it." Cue every one of us taking a selfie with an epic waterfall instead of actually seeing the damn thing. But we may be missing more than just being present in the moment.

There's a common thread for examples of spontaneously coming up with the most brilliant ideas in nature and in movement.

- Charles Darwin formed his theory of natural selection not from tinkering in a lab but from weeks wandering the Galápagos Islands, observing birds and landscapes.
- Dr. Francine Shapiro went for a walk in the park in 1987 and discovered the basis for EMDR therapy.
- Phil Knight went for an early morning run in 1962 and conceived of the concept of *play* behind Nike.

All these people were unplugged from technology. Because the kind we keep close by our sides today—iPhones and earbuds—didn't exist yet.

Often while catching up with an old friend, I start to explain what I'm doing now and typically they interrupt me and start sharing how they are already practicing the Hike to Become Challenge. What proceeds is hilarious and shocking, all at once. They go on to say some version of, "So every lunch hour, I go for a run and listen to my favorite podcast, and so I'm totally down with what you're doing."

Sigh. Not even close.

This is why I have a rule on all my hikes, whether it's a VIP 1:1 Strategy Hike or a Hike to Become®

Experience with a company or team: There are no cell phones allowed. This is the part where I normally get resistance, especially when I say, "*And your smartwatch too, please.*" Normally, executives are resistant, but it was the time at the trailhead with Grayson Sterling, a 24-year-old former college athlete turned mental performance coach, that was memorable because he said what everyone was thinking: "But how will I know how many steps I'll do?"

I laughed and reminded him that whether the watch was on or not, we'd all be getting the same number of steps in, and it was time to just enjoy the journey.

"When it's not tracking my steps, I feel like it doesn't count," he explained, perfectly capturing our modern addiction to counting everything instead of simply experiencing it.

He put his Apple Watch in my console and we headed into the woods. As Grayson later admitted: "It would have been something that I would be checking or I would be curious—oh, how far have we gone? And I would look down . . . it's so habitual that it does take your mind off of what you're focused on."

While the first two pillars are H for "hike," or walk, and I for "in nature" to get you into your genius zone, the third pillar is reminding you to keep tech off. It's not a suggestion but the damn rule. Because this one tiny change will dramatically increase or decrease the benefits of this challenge. The whole point is to disconnect with the rest of the world so you can reconnect with the one person who matters most—yourself. When you do that, you can tap into those brilliant ideas.

This is not a time to catch up with your cousin Rachel, listen to the podcast Bill just sent over, or even run to your favorite '90s hip-hop beat. If you do any of that, you are inhibiting the benefits clearly outlined in the last two chapters because your mind isn't tuning into you, it's tuning out. Most people reach for their phone not out of necessity, but out of habit, comfort, and addiction. We act like dumb animals with a serious self-awareness problem when it comes to technology. What we don't realize is what we are actually sacrificing for that tiny, short-lived dopamine hit: access to our most brilliant ideas.

Remember those sobering statistics from earlier? We're checking our phones hundreds of times daily, and Dr. Gloria Mark's research shows our attention spans have collapsed to just 47 seconds. Every notification can derail focus for up to 25 minutes. Do the math; we're basically never fully focused.

We're Afraid of Ourselves

If you take your cell phone on your daily hike, it will stop all the amazing benefits of nature and movement that turn your mind into creative genius mode. The irony? Steve Jobs, who helped bring the iPhone to life, understood this instinctively. When he was stuck on an idea, he didn't stay glued to his desk. He went for a walk, barefoot, outside. His best ideas may have come while walking in nature, not staring at screens.

Statistic after statistic and study after study highlight the dangers of technology and tell us that tech is the ultimate boogeyman. The problem that no one is talking about is what *exactly* we are avoiding every time we reach for the distraction. Could it be that we're so afraid of being alone with our thoughts that the idea of taking a walk without technology feels too damn revealing? Because it might just force us to face some uncomfortable truths. Because maybe the truth isn't out there in some big epiphany; maybe it's hiding in what we're avoiding, not what we're distracting ourselves with.

> **If you take your cell phone on your daily hike, it will stop all the amazing benefits of nature and movement that turn your mind into creative genius mode.**

I uncovered this phenomenon as I inspired hundreds of people to HIKE to find themselves again. Because when I saw how transformative this practice was for me, I couldn't help but share it with everyone. It became a weird occupational hazard. If I met you over the last year at a conference or in a hotel elevator, or even if you were my Uber driver, I would encourage you to go for a hike every day for 31 days.

Almost everyone I talked to wanted to try it. Some perfect strangers even got emotional, tearing up in a Starbucks and telling me, "This is exactly what I need in my life." Most were at a crossroads—feeling stuck, lacking clarity, unsure what's next. Just the *idea* that they could unlock some level of clarity themselves hit deep and brought on real tears on more than one occasion. Some were excited and ready to take on the challenge. Others were intimidated . . . but willing to try anyway.

But as I followed up to see how the daily hiking was going, I noticed that people fell into one of two categories: First were the people who tried for a few days and stopped, and second were the people who hiked for 31 days, or most of it, and are still hiking today. The business strategist in me grew very curious. Because I love data and research, I had to know what the difference was. So I started asking questions: Why weren't people finishing? What was holding them back? What I found was interesting. After peeling back the layers of excuses, people started to share with me that they were *afraid* to be alone with their own thoughts.

Brett Hautop, Founder of Workspace, witnessed this resistance in his workplace experiments. "At our events, we tell them ahead of time 'We're going to take your device for the day,'" he said. "Some people literally have a panic attack. Some of them won't do it."

While everyone is talking about the dangers of technology and how addictive it is, no one is talking about *why* we are constantly reaching out for the distraction. Could it be that we are afraid to be alone with our thoughts? Could it be acknowledging exactly what we are escaping each time we choose not to be present in the moment? Well, there's one way to find out. We must be brave enough to face the monster in our own mind and trust that nature is the best place for us to face these fears.

On my many hikes, I've experienced a kind of quiet that is so uncomfortable it makes your skin crawl and the hair on the back of your neck stand up. It takes all my willpower to not reach to turn on my phone. We are so used to distraction that quiet seems unnerving. Let that sink in.

What's Stalking You?

One of the questions people ask me is how I can be so comfortable hiking alone all the time. And if I'm being honest, it's never really occurred to me to be afraid. I've been a hiker most of my adult life and I'm more intimated going to a crowded event than I am on the trail.

But I had an experience that changed all of that one summer. My family and I went to explore Grand Teton National Park. It's been a bucket list item of mine for years, and so I planned a vacation the whole family would enjoy. Or so I thought. . . . This was my first time hiking in grizzly country, and I like to be prepared, so I did all the research. I learned what to expect if you encounter a bear, how black bears and grizzly bears behave differently, and, most importantly, how to deal with an unexpected encounter, like carrying bear spray and making noise to avoid surprising bears in the woods.

The first family hike was an absolute disaster. My daughter, who was four at the time and typically a good little hiker, tripped and faceplanted not even seven steps onto the trail. She was crying that she was bleeding (she wasn't), that her leg was broken (it was a scrape), and that we needed to take her to the hospital right away.

Here's a tip: If traveling in bear country, you don't need a bear bell because your toddlers are way more effective at deterring wildlife than a bell. My two-year-old insisted on screaming bloody murder from his pack, effectively scaring off all the wildlife within a 15-mile radius. I don't think we even made it in a quarter mile before my husband and I called it. Okay, back to the Airbnb. Let's find some kid-friendly activities. We came up with a plan: I'd go hiking solo after dinner and he'd go during nap time.

The next day, I headed out after dinner. There was about an hour left until sunset and I hit a trail that was off the tourist path; it was remote, and a local secret. At first, there were a few other groups on the trail, but when I reached a four-way fork in the woods, I decided to head through this gorgeous meadow and into the forest beyond. The sunlight was perfect. It was quiet and serene, and, for the first time in days, I felt at peace. As I entered the forest, it became a lot darker, with more tree coverage and a trail that was severely overgrown.

Hiking solo, I started to get these thoughts that I should turn around. Something wasn't right. . . . It occurred to me that, with the overgrowth on the trail and lack of other hikers and bikers, I could quite literally come up on a bear and scare the hell out of him. I clapped, I whistled, I hiked a few more steps, I clapped again. I told myself I was being silly and kept hiking, but this nagging feeling wouldn't go away. I needed to turn around. Cue more ridiculous clapping, throw in a whistle or two, and I kept hiking. *You need to turn around . . .* I thought. Again.

So, finally, I just decided something was off, and I turned around. Disappointed to not have hiked more than a mile or explored further, I decided it was the best course of action as I got back to the parking lot. Heading to the car, I saw the trailhead bulletin board and a sign that I somehow had missed in my excitement to get on the trail on my way in: "Warning Bear Activity in the Area." It was dated that same day. I have no idea how I missed it, because it was bright orange and the main focal point. But I tell you this story because I believe my intuition kicked in and warned me to get out of the woods that day. It didn't stop me from hiking the next morning or the days that followed, but it did remind me that, sometimes, we just need to listen to our gut.

Now, I tell you this story so you can have a good idea of my frame of mind just a few weeks later when I found myself hiking alone in the Sawtooth Mountains of Idaho. The closest town is called Stanley, with a population of 117 people. When I tell you it's remote, it's otherworldly remote. In fact, my husband and I use walkie-talkies when we go up there because most of the surrounding area is a cell phone dead zone.

The night before I was to go on the hike, I tried to recruit some of my friends to join me. One of them said, "I've read that there's been increasing bear activity in the woods. I'm out."

It's no wonder that when I loaded up the car at 5:00 a.m., there were no other lights on in their cabin. Apparently, everyone chose to sleep in. I couldn't blame them. And I always welcome the opportunity for a solo adventure.

I hit the trailhead before the sun came up. I wanted to get a majority of this hike in before my family woke up so I could spend the day with them. I saw one other hiker, with a fishing pole and a dog, headed onto the trail a few minutes before me. Other than that, there wasn't a soul for miles. At first, I was really enjoying the quiet; it was a stressful trip up. I hadn't been hiking in a few days, and it was peaceful and nice to have time alone. I went past the "Mile 1" marker and, as I was hiking farther into the woods to get to the base of the mountain range, it hit me: It was eerily quiet. Too quiet. The kind of quiet I had experienced in the Tetons when I decided to turn around.

Now, I didn't have the feeling I needed to turn around, but I felt on high alert for some reason. It was like my nervous system was remembering my other experience and couldn't quite shake it. I also couldn't help but think about my friend's comments the night before around a campfire about increased bear activity in the woods.

As I was hiking, on high alert, the forest so quiet you could literally hear a pin drop, I heard it. It was like a rustling in the bushes. It sounded bigger than a squirrel or a chipmunk, and was a little ways away. *I'm being silly*, I told myself. *It could be anything.* I kept hiking. If there was a bear in the area, I would surely know. I would feel it. As I kept hiking, I heard the noise again. This time it sounded closer. Okay, now I was really freaked out. My heart started racing and I felt my hands get clammy. My eyes were looking ahead, but my brain was behind me, worried about what was stalking me in the woods.

The problem was, at this point, I was about two miles into my hike. I pulled out my backpack to get out my walkie-talkie to tell my husband what was going on, and that's when I realized, in my hurry to get on the trail early, I left the damn thing at home.

Now I had two problems: (1) There was something stalking me in the woods, and (2) I couldn't tell anyone about it or even give my location. OK, two problems and two potential courses of action:

1. I could turn around. But whatever it was, it was behind me. So I would either scare it off or run into it. I didn't like those odds.
2. I could keep hiking, putting as much distance between myself and the stalker as possible and hopefully catching up with the fishing guy and his dog.

I decided to hike on. I liked those odds better than the idea of running face-first into a bear. I hiked for another mile and heard nothing. Whew. My plan had worked. The stalker had given up. I stopped by a tree to take a sip of water. I didn't want to delay too long, just in case I was putting more distance between me and whatever was behind me. As I put my water bottle back into my bag, I heard a similar noise. At first, I flinched, but then

I realized the sound wasn't coming from behind me at all. . . . It was coming from my backpack.

I thought, *Wait a minute. It cannot be . . . there's no way. I'm not that stupid.* To test my sinking feeling, I packed up my stuff, trying to remember how I had it placed when I started, and hit the trail again. And that's when I heard the noise. But this time I knew for sure . . . I was absolutely ridiculous. It wasn't a damn bear stalking me. It was my half-empty water bottle sloshing around. The way I had it packed made a strange noise that sounded just like bushes rustling behind me. That's what had scared the hell out of me for the last two and a half miles.

That's the thing about fear. It can be spot-on, warning you to avoid a situation, like it did for me in the Grand Tetons. But most of the time, fear is just like a half-empty water bottle, scaring you for two and a half miles, making you question your life choices, and warning how good you'll taste to a bear—when it's really just a sound coming from your own backpack.

The problem with technology on the trail is that it keeps you from entering the uncomfortable space of your own mind. It's a constant distraction, keeping you disconnected from the part of your brain you need to access the most.

We spend most of our lives running from what we *think* is a bear chasing us in the woods—but often it's just a half-empty water bottle scaring you out of having your life's greatest adventures.

You might be thinking of a massive career change, but you worry it will destroy everything you've built. You're terrified of a leap of faith because the economic time isn't right. You are worried that you're not cut out for the new promotion or ready to take on a new audacious challenge. This is the part where you need to ask yourself, *Is my imposter syndrome a real grizzly bear, or just some water sloshing around in my backpack?*

> **You'll never know the difference unless you embrace the quiet and the crazy of your own thoughts.**

You'll never know the difference unless you embrace the quiet and the crazy of your own thoughts.

Just remember to pack the bear spray.

7

Every Day: For 31 Days

When I challenged myself to hike for 31 days, it was totally random. I'm hyper competitive with myself and I knew I needed something easy to hold me accountable to actually do it. That day was December 23, 2023. I thought, *If January has 31 days, I could hike for a whole month, couldn't I?* I also thought back to the two other times in my life where I had lost my way.

Losing Myself

Back in 2013, I found myself trapped in a marriage I had no business being in. Shortly after marrying my first husband, I found out he had a crushing addiction problem that he hid—even from me. And that was easy to do, because I was a workaholic. I gave everything to my career and put my personal life on autopilot. When he asked me to marry him, I ignored my gut reaction and the red flags, and instead of saying no, I just added it to my to-do list. Until the honeymoon brought forth a truth that even I couldn't escape from—I didn't want to be married to him. He was not my life partner. And I had unwittingly just legally and financially tied myself to someone who, for the next year and half, was going to drain everything I had in order to fight an addiction that wasn't mine. I found myself hiking regularly in Ridley Creek State Park, close to my home in Pennsylvania, to escape the tension in the house. After several weeks, I wasn't just escaping the tension. I had found myself again. Alone, unplugged, in movement, and in nature, I remembered how to breathe clearly again. With that came my ability to think clearly and see that I had my whole life ahead of me, and I had a choice to make. I chose me.

After choosing to take back my life, I spent the next several years unattached and aspiring to do things I never dreamt possible before—hiking daily, taking up adventures, and eventually meeting my current husband, Steve. We moved to the beautiful Pacific Northwest, settling in Portland for my role working in Global Accounts so I could be closer to the Fortune 10 clients in my portfolio. At first, it was a dream. I was traveling the world, closing big deals, and exploring our new home state. Then in March of 2020, Steve and I welcomed our daughter, Brynn, into the world, and everything I thought I knew was about to change. We became new parents two weeks before the global pandemic, which left us isolated from friends and family, and any sort of support network.

A few short months later, I found myself coming back from maternity leave at the height of the remote work insanity. Due to voluntary separations and two global team members leaving, I returned to discover I was now responsible for three additional Fortune 500 clients—including one of the world's most valuable companies and several other tech giants. This was on top of my existing workload, which included some of the most recognizable global brands in the world—think smiley face boxes and fruit logos.

My job was to create strategic plans for elevating these vendor relationships into true business partnerships, then manage a global salesforce to execute those plans. Here I was, a new mom on the West Coast, isolated from friends and family on the East Coast, with a whole country and a global pandemic between us. I did the only thing I knew how to do: I threw myself into the work.

Every day became like *Groundhog Day*. I'd wake at 3:00 a.m. to nurse my daughter, then wake again at 4:30 a.m. for a Teams call, and the next 16 to 18 hours became a blur of back-to-back Zoom and Teams calls, emails, WhatsApp texts, eating lactation cookies at my desk, breaking for the occasional meal with my family, and then getting back online to chat with colleagues in India and China after bathtime. Often I'd find myself falling into bed at 11:00 p.m. or later. It wasn't sustainable, it wasn't healthy, but I couldn't see the forest through the trees.

Until one day, while waiting for my sixth Zoom call of the day, I looked out my office window and saw the treetops of Forest Park, one of the largest urban parks in the entire United States. It was one of the reasons we'd moved to Portland, Oregon, for my new role in Global Accounts—the ability to be on a hiking trail within ten minutes. Then it hit me with crushing sadness: I couldn't remember the last time I'd been hiking. It was like I was seeing a long-lost friend for the first time in years. I cancelled my next Zoom call and drove to the trailhead, instinctively being pulled into the woods. I left my cell phone in the car and just walked. After about 10 minutes, I started breathing in a way that made me realize I had been holding my breath for months. After about 20 minutes, I realized how peaceful I felt. I couldn't hear the incessant dings of my cellphone, or hear my daughter crying and feel the insane mom guilt that the nanny would have to get her, because mommy was too busy working. I felt like me again. And it had been a while. When I got back to the car, I made up my mind to keep showing up on the trail. Even if I had to schedule it into my workday.

The balance of 2020 was filled with busy remote workdays, solo hikes, neighborhood walks, and finding a way back to myself again. I found a way to be more creative and productive in my work. I started to achieve balance. I came up with some really great ideas for the accounts I was managing, most of which happened on the hiking trail. That year, I was even given the Regional Vice President of Global & Strategic Accounts of the Year award for achieving double-digit growth. From the outside looking in, I was crushing it, and finally found balance with my work. But underneath it all . . . something else was simmering.

Through hiking daily, I reached a point of clarity that my family was truly unhappy in Portland. While in love with the nature and the land, we missed our community and our family, and we wanted to raise our daughter in a place that reminded us of our own childhoods. But we were trapped by my corporate career. I had spent decades building up to this point, earning my MBA, traveling the world, closing multimillion-dollar deals. If I stayed, my future looked bright—from the outside. But my quality of life was diminishing, and somewhere in the back of my mind was the reminder that being Powerfully Present with those you love the most is what truly matters. Nature taught me that my career doesn't define me. I do. One day, I simply asked my husband if he wanted to move. His entire face lit up—he'd been having similar thoughts, but wanted to keep supporting me in my career. So he'd kept most of it to himself, until my daily hikes taught me there's more to life than working around the clock and being labeled successful on someone else's terms. In early 2022, two years after hiking regularly, I quit my corporate role and walked away from it all. It seemed crazy. I left behind my network, we moved to a different state, and I walked away from an industry I had spent decades in. It scared the hell out of me. But what scared me even more was the idea that I might never find the thing that would truly light me up.

I took a remote role at a start-up company just to support our move to Boise, Idaho. One weekend, on a friend's suggestion, we flew to Boise to check it out, and within three days we fell in love with the epic views of mountain ranges, the access to nature, and, above all else, the people. Boise is a special place you must experience to understand. It's filled with community, love, and people who genuinely want to raise kids together and support each other. We had found our new home, with both community and a laid-back lifestyle that included getting out in nature regularly. With all the changes going on, I also found out we were expecting our second child.

> **But what scared me even more was the idea that I might never find the thing that would truly light me up.**

One July morning I woke up, six months pregnant and with our house under construction, to a dreaded email stating, "Your role has been eliminated, alongside 54 others." My work laptop had been remotely shut off and I had a meeting with HR in two hours. In reality, I loved their mission, but hated the job. But this was our only income, and my husband was waiting to be brought back to his job that same summer.

I proceeded to interview with everyone in my network I could think of—but due to being six months pregnant and disclosing it in the interview process, I witnessed time and time again that when it came time for the offer letter, a company would suddenly want to wait until the following year, or had convenient budget cuts for the role I was applying for. I knew in my heart I wasn't comfortable not disclosing my pregnancy, as I would be starting a job and soon after need to take maternity leave. But the shocking amount of resistance and, quite frankly, pregnancy discrimination that I faced was sobering.

What I didn't do at this moment was hike. Being six months pregnant in the height of Idaho summers, which can often go beyond 100 degrees, I somehow conveniently forgot the one thing that had always brought me clarity. But luckily, I had my husband, Steve. One day, he took me by the shoulders and said, "Just stop. Stop interviewing. It's making you miserable. You've always wanted to own your own company; it's why you went back to school to get your MBA in the first place. I believe in you. Now is the time."

My jaw hit the floor. At six months pregnant, under contract for building a new house, a toddler at home, and no income coming in for either of us, I thought, *Are you insane? Now is definitely not the time.* But he just said, "I believe in you."

Later that week, he helped me file to create DeAngelo Consulting and a new website. I buckled in for entrepreneurial life, only to find myself very close to burnout again on top of that foothill on December 23, 2023. Because the problem was never corporate America. The problem was not the countless Zoom calls or the demanding clients. The problem wasn't trying to manage teams from a variety of cultures around a common goal. The problem wasn't the long hours or the insane workload. The problem wasn't the roller coaster of building a business and establishing a brand, or having to be a jack of all trades. The problem was *me*.

Why 31 Days?

This time, I knew what to do—go out into nature and find clarity, or at least a trail map to find it again. So, on top of the hill, I thought, *What if I just hiked for 31 days straight to find myself again?*

What I set as an arbitrary goal because January has 31 days, ironically worked out well. Because James Clear, author of *Atomic Habits*—someone I'd call the king of tiny habits, found that it takes at least 18 days to form a simple habit, but 21 to 30 days for complex behavioral changes.

The most common question I get asked about this part is: What if I don't have 30 minutes in my day? Here's the answer: First, everyone has 30 minutes in their day; it's about what you're willing to sacrifice for it. Second—if you've been paying attention—this one small daily practice will skyrocket your productivity and boost your creativity, making you way more focused on what you really need to do. I want you to think of this challenge as medicine for your body, a detox for your mind, and a cold plunge to remember who you are again.

Together, these four elements create a powerful reset for your overworked brain: (1) Movement activates new neural pathways and (2) nature calms your nervous system, (3) leaving tech behind eliminates constant interruptions, and (4) daily practice ensures that clarity, not confusion, is your new default.

Whenever I work with people now, the Hike to Become Challenge is part of their journey. For my one-on-one coaching clients, their Hike to Become Challenge starts the day of the VIP hike. I guide them to use the next 30 days to hike alone, unplugged, with only their thoughts and a field guide to jot down anything pivotal to share with me later. The ideas my clients come up with are clear, inspiring, and overwhelmingly exciting. I encourage them to share these thoughts with me via a walkie-talkie app that we use to connect in between coaching sessions (obviously, once they are done with the hike). One of my favorite things is sipping coffee in the morning and listening to my client's early morning hike breakthroughs.

When I work with corporate groups, I start with a campfire chat or keynote speech, followed by either a Powerfully Present guided hike, which includes forest bathing and grounding elements, or a Radically Self-Aware Adventure Hike to test the limits of their bodies and their minds. But that's just Day 1. For the next 30 days, all team members participate in the Hike to Become Challenge on their own remotely, and are encouraged to enlist a hiking accountability buddy to keep them on track. John Finch, CEO of The Legacy Group and the first executive brave enough to let me take his entire team hiking mid-keynote, discovered how this approach can change workplace habits.

"It's become normal," he said. "'Hey, you want to go for a walk? Let's take a stroll and chat.' It gets you out of the office and into a different environment, which allows you to let down your guard and have more simple conversations. Nature is a powerful elixir for opening people up and relaxing them to a degree where they feel they can maybe be more vulnerable. Out in the open, there's something that opens up the pores, opens up your mind.'"

While not everyone can get through the first week or so of learning to be Powerfully Present with themselves on the trail, the ones who embrace it find beauty on the other side. I've heard stories of people who used the Hike to Become Challenge to give up addictive behaviors, grieve lost loved ones, and even find space to process feelings they didn't know they had. This is a powerful tool. The best part is that it's free, and almost anyone can do it.

With the four elements of HIKE and a 31-day commitment, you now hold something in your hands that can change the trajectory of your life, open possibilities you didn't know existed, and even spark your most innovative ideas. The reason for consistency is to give you a tool that will last you the rest of your life. But let's start with 31 days.

From Crazy Idea to Business Innovation

Back to the business case for 31 days. . . . I didn't decide to take my clients hiking during my own Hike to Become Challenge on Day 1, or even Day 7. It was somewhere in the messy middle between Day 15 and Day 21 that a wild idea struck me on a trail: *Why don't I take my clients hiking?* Since bringing this into my work, my business revenue has tripled and I've brought on an incredibly smart hike experience coordinator to help me manage the workload. What started as DeAngelo Consulting is now Hike to Become—a magnetic brand that stops people in their tracks and makes them ask,

"Wait . . . you hike with executives to unlock wild business ideas?"

My own Hike to Become Challenge, which had everything to do with my own journey, has now gone on to inspire a TEDx Talk, this book, and countless people to HIKE to find themselves again. And I'm not done. But don't take my word for it. There are many examples of brilliant business minds in this book who have used a similar method to tackle their biggest challenges and unlock their brightest ideas. And it wasn't one hike, one run, one walk in the woods—it was a habit. A default to seek clarity in nature that kept them on course to understand the three biggest questions humans face: Who am I? Why am I here? And, of course, What am I going to do about it?

In his book, *Shoe Dog*, Phil Knight recounts a time when he was contemplating giving up his dream to travel the world, live a life of *play*, and bring Japanese running shoes to the market in America. He found himself living a dream life in Hawaii, staying longer than he thought he would, until he felt the urgent pull to get back to the plan. But when he approached his traveling companion to hit the road again, he found his friend had decided to stay in Hawaii for a girl he had met. He was content to live the life he had found there. Feeling lost, Phil went for a walk on the beach and, not surprisingly, found some clarity. Here is an excerpt from his book *Shoe Dog*:

"'Game over,' I told myself. The last thing I wanted to do was pack up and return to Oregon. But I couldn't see traveling around the world alone, either. Go home, a faint inner voice told me. Get a normal job. Be a normal person. Then I heard another faint voice, equally emphatic. No, don't go home. Keep going. Don't stop."

I've heard that faint voice too . . . but mine sounded more like "It might be crazy, but it's worth a try." So I want to ask you: What's stopping you from meeting the one person who matters most on the trail . . . yourself?

8

Your Brain on Nature

Why Getting Outside Matters

What happens after the Hike to Become Challenge? Most people, myself included, continue to incorporate this practice into their daily life. The Hike to Become Challenge is like a cold plunge for your mind, a chance to get to know "you" again. After those initial days, people who have finished the challenge just tend to keep on hiking. It may not be every day, but most continue practicing the HIKE methodology at least three to four times a week.

One of the biggest challenges I find is that, while I hike with clients, it doesn't have the same effect as the deeply personal practice of doing it by myself. It's good, and what I love to do, but I'm facilitating an amazing experience *for them*. My focus is on everyone else. When I practice alone, it allows me sacred space to just . . . think. As Bryant Richardson, founder and president of Real Blue Sky and one of the first Hike to Become Challenge participants to finish the full month, told me: "This practice has given me the space to process feelings I didn't realize I had."

I couldn't agree more. I've experienced so many moments on the trail where a problem I was wrestling with just disappeared. I realized the problem may have seemed like a mountain, but once I got out there and hiked, it vanished—because I found the mental perspective to just let it go. I realized between rocks and sagebrush that what I was worried about actually didn't matter at all.

Then there are the "Aha!" ideas that hit me—things that came out of nowhere and felt like divine inspiration: the concept behind this book, most of my TEDx Talk, solutions for clients—there have been countless examples of great ideas that hit me once I made this practice part of my life. Between letting go of the noise and discovering great ideas, I found the clarity to focus only on what matters, the energy to be insanely productive on the stuff that actually does matter, and the creativity to come up with wild ideas in my work. And that made all the difference in the world. Work started to feel like fun again. Gone were the days of feeling like I was on autopilot and uninspired. Now not only do I love what I do, I have become part of the process. It feels like magic.

But, as with most magical phenomena, there's science behind it.

Searching for a Scientist

For over 18 months, I had been hiking with clients using a technique I cobbled together based on my own experiences and any scientific research I could get my hands on. I knew it worked; I just wasn't quite sure how.

That's when I found Dr. David Strayer's work. As a professor of cognition and neural science at the University of Utah, and an avid hiker and rafter, David is one of the few experts in the country studying the effects that nature has on our brain. His research also explores attention, multitasking, and distracted driving. He's remarkably hard to get a hold of, which is very on brand. He doesn't do social media, most of his email addresses are outdated, and if he's not out in nature figuring out ways to put electrodes on someone's brain, he's probably in the lab or driving (tech-free) to immerse himself in nature.

But he's the one person I knew could help me understand the phenomenon I was seeing—in both myself and my clients. I sent emails, I called the University of Utah's hotline—which rerouted me to the hospital psych ward at least five times—but I couldn't seem to track down the elusive scientist who studies our brains on nature.

While I had fantasized about how cool it would be to interview him while on an actual hike, I was slowly starting to doubt my chances of even reaching him. I put out a request on social media, asking if anyone knew Dr. David Strayer or could help me find a way to contact him. I sent a silent prayer out to the universe, and just like that, within two days, I had three people come to my rescue. One found his personal cell phone number. I did what most people don't do anymore: I just called him. The timing was perfect, because he wasn't driving or rafting in the middle of a river somewhere and picked up the phone. I probably sounded crazy as I introduced myself, while trying to simultaneously explain that I was not a stalker or a telemarketer, and asked him for the interview for this book. Luckily for me, he said yes.

During our time together, David shared insights that confirmed everything I was seeing and more. At the end of the interview, I may have even volunteered myself to someday be a research participant, even offering to hike with some electrodes on my brain.

The Science Behind the Magic

David's work provides key insights on what nature immersion can do for the brain. In 2012, he and his colleagues organized a study using participants in Outward Bound wilderness programs. They found that people who spent four days backpacking in nature, disconnected entirely from electronic devices, were up to 50 percent more creative than their counterparts who had yet to hit the trailhead. The participants were 56 adults with an average

age of 28 who engaged in four- to six-day wilderness hikes. They were divided into two groups: One group took a remote associates test (a standard measure of creative problem-solving) before their hike started (average score of 4.04), while the second group took the test after four days of hiking unplugged (average score of 6.08).

While fascinating, this study cannot scientifically prove that nature, movement, and unplugging are the root cause because they didn't test the same subjects before and after the hike. David and team acknowledged this limitation, stating, "It would be useful in future research to administer the Remote Associates Test both before and after the hike to the same individuals." But even with this oversight, this pivotal study provides a glimpse into something we all instinctively already know: We are way more creative and good at problem-solving when we are in movement, in nature, and without the distraction of technology.

The Evolutionary Clash

As we kicked off the interview, I shared the background of why I was trying to write a book to inspire people to change the way we work, our relationship with nature, and ultimately ourselves. I told David I wanted to start a movement to get more people out of the office, off technology, and into their boldest business ideas. And then I sat back and learned from the master.

David has spent his career studying two key areas: distracted driving and our brains on nature. What I wanted was some credibility for the concepts in this book. What I got was a masterclass in how our brains actually work, and how the modern clash between our evolutionary wiring and today's technology has completely severed our access to our most creative and innovative ideas.

"We've surrounded ourselves with an artificial environment that is completely the opposite of the natural environment of our evolutionary history," David explained. "Our brains have not evolved to be in the environment that we live in now."

The iPhone came out in 2007, and since then, everything changed. We now have what David calls a "portal to pretty much anything you can do" constantly attached to us. The problem, he says, is that "when you get bombarded as much as we do with technology, it tends to overtax our brains, because our brains weren't designed to interact with all that stuff hitting us all the time." This is why we feel like we're on chronic overload.

The Four Attentional Networks

David explained that we have four different attentional networks that evolved to keep us alive. These networks are old and adaptive. The problem is that people engineering this technology have hijacked our evolutionary responses in a way that keeps us constantly paying attention to what they want: Think cell phone notifications. This all keeps us from tapping into our default mode, where creative thinking thrives. But to understand how to prevent this, let's first explore how these networks have biologically evolved to focus our attention for better or for worse.

1. Alerting Network – "Always On" Mode

Purpose: This network is always on, constantly scanning for potential threats and triggering the fight-or-flight response, which is your sympathetic nervous system.

How it works: Let's pretend that right now you're lying in a magical meadow in the middle of a forest, reading the best book you've ever held, but your alerting mode is still scanning for threats.

Problem: While this is useful if there's a wild animal about to eat you, it's totally not useful during your modern workday, because your phone's notifications are engineered to trigger this ancient safety mechanism. Every buzz, ping, and alert hijacks your brain into thinking there's a threat, keeping you in chronic high-alert mode. No wonder we are all severely stressed out.

2. Orienting Network – "Look Here! Now Look There!"

Purpose: This network directs your attention to specific things in space and time. It responds to "sudden onsets," like snaps, growls, honks, beeps, or rings.

How it works: Let's say, as you're reading this amazing book in a meadow, you hear a growl behind you. Now your brain snaps to attention and you swivel your head to see what is in the bushes to figure out where it came from and what it is . . . that is orienting you to the situation and just how freaked out you should or shouldn't be.

Problem: Modern life bombards you with competing alerts that change and confuse your orienting network. While you're trying to get shit done, constant notifications like emails, Teams chats, LinkedIn notifications, and calendar invites pop up. Your brain frantically orients from one "urgent" thing to another, fragmenting your focus. None of these digital interruptions are actual emergencies, but your brain can't tell the difference.

3. **Executive Attentional Network – "Think Hard, Stay Focused"**

Purpose: This network powers decision-making, problem-solving, creativity, and something most of us lack—impulse control.

How it works: The prefrontal cortex, basically your brain's CEO, manages complex thinking, such as what to do if you are in the meadow, hear a growl, and identify it's a mountain lion ready to pounce. Your "Executive Attention Network" takes over and helps you think through what to do next. This is helpful when your life is on the line. Ironically, this same network helps you control your impulses to check your phone 44 times a minute. Unfortunately, it rarely can, because you're always stuck in orienting or alerting mode.

Problem: Constantly switching between alerts and distractions fatigues this network, like overusing a muscle. When depleted, you struggle to concentrate, make good decisions, and think strategically. This is the part of your brain responsible for your best business ideas.

4. Default Mode Network – "Creative and Reflective Mode"

Purpose: This is "unfocused attention," like daydreaming. There is no task at hand; you're allowing your brain to wander. Default mode unlocks breakthrough insights, strategic thinking, and innovative ideas.

How it works: Let's go back to the meadow and take the book and the mountain lion away. Now you are hiking along, just watching the trees sway in the breeze. This experience activates your "soft fascination," which is deeply restorative for your brain. It happens as you stare at campfires, flowing water, or leaves blowing in the wind. It also requires something even rarer than a sober Sasquatch sighting—the boredom and the quiet to come alive.

Problem: This network needs exactly what modern life rarely provides: uninterrupted time without hard stimulation. You know, like lying in a meadow (without the book) and just staring at the sky. No mountain lion is present. Your most innovative ideas live here, but your inability to access them, due to the hijacking of the other attentional networks and our tech addiction, is the real problem.

The HIKE Solution

The magic behind the HIKE methodology is simple: By hiking alone and unplugged, you give your alerting and orienting networks a break. After 30 to 40 minutes, your executive network begins to restore, and your default mode network finally comes alive.

"The prefrontal cortex acts in a sense like a muscle, and can be overused," David explained. "When it's overused, it can't be as efficient. If you go into nature and set aside technology for a little while, you recalibrate and let that part of the brain rest."

The problem with our modern-day reality is that we are bombarded with things that grab our attention by force, what environmental psychologists Rachel and Stephen Kaplan call "hard fascination." That includes computer screens, social media feeds, television, or even a city walk with bright lights, beeping car horns, and traffic. These things all require directed attention, focus, and the ability to filter out distractions to stay on task, or not get run over by a car.

In contrast, the Default Mode Network needs what the Kaplans' research refers to as "soft fascination." Rather than hijacking your attention, soft fascination gently engages it. Think flowing rivers, flickering campfires, rustling trees—all stimuli that hold your attention just enough to let your brain rest and wander, often sparking creative thought. Their research unpacks an idea called *attention restoration theory*, also known as "your brain needs a damn break."

David described it in action: "You can stare at a fire that's just flickering for hours. There's a lot of new information there, right? It's warm, and it's got a glow, but you can stare at it for hours and hours because it's got that kind of movement. That's soft fascination. Same thing with looking at rivers and oceans and trees—the leaves blowing in the wind."

This is exactly what happens during your HIKE practice. The gentle movement in nature creates the perfect environment and soft fascination for your Default Mode Network to come alive. "The thinking is that [soft fascination] releases the Executive Attentional Network so it can rest. It activates the default meditative mindfulness, a kind of in-the-moment type of network," David said.

Here's what no one talks about: This beautiful network needs quiet and boredom to activate.

Guess what's in high demand these days? Exactly—boredom and quiet. Our constant tech addiction has kept us from accessing our most creative, innovative ideas, and frankly, no one is talking about it.

That's why your best ideas hit you in the shower, because it's one of the few places you don't take your phone. You are forced into boredom and silence while you're sudsing up. But showers last ten minutes. The HIKE method gives you 30 to 45 minutes of that same cognitive freedom, dramatically increasing your chances of breakthrough thinking.

> **Our constant tech addiction has kept us from accessing our most creative, innovative ideas, and frankly, no one is talking about it.**

Seeing it Work in Real Time

David's research shows exactly why the HIKE methodology works. In controlled studies, he found that people who spent time in nature without technology showed dramatically different brain patterns than those who brought their phones along. He talks about this study in his TEDx Talk "Restore Your Brain with Nature." He divided participants into two groups: One group walked in an arboretum, unplugged; the other made phone calls to friends while walking the same path. The results were striking: The unplugged group showed clear neural signatures of cognitive restoration, while the phone group's brains remained in the same overtaxed state they started with.

"When you're walking without the cell phone, you can kind of just be in the flow," David noted. But add technology? "They're switching their attention back and forth, and consequently, you're overusing the parts of the brain most associated with creativity."

Even more revealing was what happened to perception. When David asked participants what they remembered from their walk, those who had been on their phones were "a little bit clueless," as he put it. "They don't know. When they're walking and talking, they're not actually looking and seeing some of the things that are right in front of them."

This phenomenon, called "inattentional blindness," explains why so many breakthrough solutions seem to come out of nowhere when we're in nature. The solutions aren't new—they were always there. We just couldn't see them because our overtaxed brains were too busy switching between alerts to notice what was right in front of us.

David explained that "if you're trying to basically pick up some kind of pattern or trend in the data to your business world and trying to . . . make decisions you might need to make, and you're just multitasking, you might actually miss things that are right in front of you, that someone who isn't multitasking will catch right away."

I witnessed this transformation firsthand at the Conscious Investor Growth Summit in Coeur d'Alene, Idaho. During one of the VIP guided hikes, I asked everyone to pair up with someone they didn't already know to practice being Powerfully Present with another human being. Dakota Barney was one of the hikers who found the courage to explore a wild idea with a perfect stranger. I stopped the group throughout our hike and shared what metrics we were crossing. Once we hit the point where cognitive function would be more activated, I asked the group to share their wildest business idea, the one they'd always thought was too crazy or silly, with their hiking partner. I told the hiking partners their only job was to hold space for the other person's wild idea and explore the possibilities. It created a dramatic moment for Dakota and unlocked an idea that had been "deep buried in the basement," as he later told me, something he'd "blown off for the whole year."

But after 30 minutes of walking unplugged in nature, something shifted. "When you do it, you break away. You can really dig deep," Dakota explained. "Maybe soul searching, maybe just learning more about who you are, maybe aligning with your purpose."

For the first time, Dakota shared his vision of creating a faith-based program to develop young boys into men through outdoor experiences and leadership practices.

"When you're speaking your truth, and you get that inspirational vibe—I felt that pretty hard a couple times while I was speaking," Dakota reflected. "I was like, well, maybe there is something to this idea that I have."

His wife, Jen, witnessed the transformation from the group circle where we shared our wild ideas by the lake prior to forest bathing. "I've never seen Dakota push through that wall," she told me later. "And it happened while we were there, and it was a very huge deal. I went into this conference hoping that would happen for him—that he would get a little more clarity on which direction to go, just because, in certain ways, we've been stuck."

When I asked Dakota if this breakthrough could have happened in a conference room, his response was emphatic: "A hundred percent not at all. Trying to think about having that conversation inside in a conference room—not being in the dirt, not breathing nature, not flowing—I don't think it would have been as deep or as thoughtful."

The science explains exactly what happened. Dakota's default mode network finally came alive after being suppressed by constant distractions. His buried idea wasn't new at all; it had been there all along, waiting for the right cognitive conditions and the right encouragement to surface.

The transformation didn't end on the trail. Dakota went on a 16-mile solo hike the following Saturday to think deeper about his vision. Within days, he'd called a friend who wanted to help organize a trial run with their sons. The "buried" idea had become an actionable business plan, all because his brain finally had the space to access its own creative potential.

To finally finish this book, I hid myself away in a cabin in the woods for a few days to write. When it was time for a break and a caffeine refuel, I remembered a recent conversation with an old work colleague who mentioned that his childhood best friend owned a bakery in McCall, Idaho, called Paikka, which in Finnish means "gathering place." A coffee craving led me to a chance meeting with Christian Toebe, the childhood friend who does more than just run a bakery and a regenerative farm with his wife, Jessica. Christian is also the COO of Bovino & Associates law firm. He was kind enough to give me a tour of the farm, and through our conversations, I realized the universe had a grand plan in my meeting him.

I was fascinated by the dichotomy between his two worlds: managing a law firm and spending time building a farm while raising a family. During our chat, he shared with me that "seventy-five percent of my business ideas happen while I'm outside and unplugged." For Christian, nature isn't just a break from work, it's essential to his work. "I view the nature portion of it as a need that is not widely accepted as a need," he explained. "I am not the best employee, I'm not the best farmer, if I'm not fulfilling that need."

When Christian explained why he thinks this works, I couldn't help but think of the correlations to his theory and bilateral stimulation in action.

"There's this line down the middle of the body," he said, "called the mid-sagittal plane. When I cross that plane, whether it's being hypnotized or what have you, I feel like I reach this other state. And it's the same thing with running, or Nordic skiing, or hiking, or walking—my body is crossing that mid-sagittal plane, and I do feel like I reach some level of meditation."

The wild ideas and great solutions to problems speak for themselves. While working on his farm, Christian designed the entire organizational chart for his law firm. On the chairlift with his snowboarding buddy, they developed their business plan for a tiny house village that "would solve just so many issues" for affordable housing. During a challenging run, he figured out a client management system for handling hundreds of legal cases with just six employees. "I was actually out on the farm at that point, and I had to run inside and write it down really quick," he recalled.

"When that nature need is being met, it allows my brain to go to these other places that I might not consider if I was sitting in a room by myself or behind a desk somewhere," Christian explained.

"There's nothing occupying that part of your brain that's just in that day-to-day grind. That's now opened up to allow other things in."

The science backs up what Christian experiences. When his basic survival needs are met, and he's in nature and in movement, his default mode network activates, accessing the innovative thinking that just wouldn't happen if he was stuck in a cubicle or behind his home office desk.

The Missing Piece

But knowing the science isn't enough. Understanding that your brain craves the gentle stimulation of soft fascination won't change your life until you're willing to step away from the societal rules that tell us work is only happening in the office, behind a desk, and plugged into technology. Dakota's advice rings true: "You gotta turn the noise off. . . . You have to be alone to sit with your thoughts, and if you speak them out loud, it helps bring clarity. If you always have the noise on, and you can't have the space, you'll never hear it. You'll never be guided."

What's stopping you from doing the same thing that unlocks innovative ideas like Christian, Dakota, or any others featured in this book? Honestly, nothing. All you need to do is to reframe your relationship with work, ditch the iPhone, and pick up your hiking boots.

The Mountain in Your Mind

9

Becoming Fearless

What Really Scares Us

Once you've committed to the Hike to Become Challenge, I want to prepare you for what's next. Because it sounds like a walk in the park, but I can assure you—it's not. Just like any good trail, it's best to have a map and a hint of what you're in for. As your guide, it's only fair of me to prepare you for the terrain ahead.

Starting the Hike to Become Challenge is only part of the journey. Once you're on the trail, you'll come to the base of what I call "Climbing the Mountain in Your Mind," and that's when the real work begins. Half the battle is showing up on the trail. The other half is embracing the journey and what happens next. As I've experienced this myself and led others on the

> **Once you're on the trail, you'll come to the base of what I call "Climbing the Mountain in Your Mind," and that's when the real work begins.**

adventure, I've noticed three key elements emerge when Climbing the Mountain in Your Mind:

1. At the base of the mountain, you must Become Fearless—challenging yourself to show up.
2. As you start climbing the most difficult elevations, you develop Radical Self-Awareness.
3. And as you ascend to the peak of the summit, you cultivate Powerful Presence.

This is a journey, and an adventure to rediscover who you really are, why you are here, and how to show up as that person in your life and your work. If you're lucky, part of this process will include unlocking your *Wild Advantage*.

One of the first things I experienced through my own Hike to Become Challenge was forcing myself to sit with my uncomfortable thoughts. Just like I experienced on the trail when I came up with the idea, limiting beliefs, imposter syndrome, and all of those unkind things we say to ourselves start creeping in, which is why we don't often sit (or hike) alone with our own thoughts. But here's why we need to push past that point: Once we get comfortable with the uncomfortable, something magical happens. When we aren't distracted by other people, to-do lists, or technology, we can come to our own rescue. The ideas that we daydream about start to take root and we *fight* for them instead of dismissing them. I call this entering into Becoming

Fearless, because when we walk alone, we start to remember how truly badass we are. Nature has this profound effect on us. But we have to be brave enough to take the first step.

If we are going to face our greatest fear of what being alone with our own thoughts can reveal to us, it's a good idea to do it in a place that melts our stress and anxiety and enhances our emotional well-being. And once our brain is activated, we can process the information at a deeper level, allowing for space to understand ourselves and our lives, and how we are showing up in it.

Now, if being afraid to sit alone with your own thoughts sounds silly to you, there's scientific evidence to back it up, and the results are quite literally shocking. A study out of the University of Virginia asked over 400 participants to be alone in a room with nothing to distract them, except . . . you guessed it . . . their own thoughts. There were only two rules:

1. They couldn't fall asleep (this was a bunch of college students).
2. They couldn't leave the room for approximately 6 to 15 minutes.

Before the experiment began, researchers gave the participants a sample electric shock and explained they could choose to press a button and shock themselves again during the thinking period if they wanted to keep busy. Here's the wild part: 72 percent said they didn't like the shock and would pay to avoid it.

And yet . . . when left alone?

At least 50 percent of participants still shocked themselves.

Specifically, 67 percent of men and 25 percent of women opted to press that button.

The results of the study show that, in our modern world, where we use being "busy" as currency, and are always looking for the next distraction, the idea of being alone with our own thoughts is more terrifying than actual physical pain.

While we see this in our personal life, choosing to doomscroll over being present, the problem of checking out also happens in our work. If we are truly honest with ourselves, how often do we choose mindless meetings over strategic thinking? We desperately fill our calendars to avoid facing difficult situations, like letting go of a key employee whose sales numbers are phenomenal but who is toxic to the health of the team. Why deal with it? Because, after all, human beings are masters of deflection, and the hard choices are, well, hard.

While everyone is talking about the dangers of technology and how addictive it is, no one is talking about *why* we are constantly reaching out for the distraction. Could it be that we are afraid to be alone with our thoughts? Could it be acknowledging exactly what we are escaping from each time we choose not to be present in the moment? Well, there's one way to find out. We must be brave enough to face the monster in our own mind and trust that nature is the best place for us to face these fears.

Most people think the part you must be fearless about is close to the summit, and that's where they are wrong. The part you must be the most fearless about is on Day 1—making the commitment to step onto the trail that leads you to the Mountain in Your Mind in the first place.

Nature Reveals What Boardrooms Hide

Before clients work with me, I send out an intake form and ask them a variety of questions, including what's their greatest fear—the thing that keeps them up at night. I get variety of answers:

- "Lack of cashflow."
- "The state of the economy."
- "That I'll provide a product/service that isn't good enough."
- "Not being able to pivot in my career."

What's fascinating to me is that, on every hike I take people on, between miles two and three, when defenses are down and pretenses have fallen away, I ask the same question: "What's your greatest fear . . . the thing that keeps you up at night?"

And you know what? The answers are always different from my client's intake form, yet the same as everyone else on the trail. It's some version of:

- "I'm not good enough."
- "I don't have anything valuable to say."
- "My ideas don't matter."
- "What if they find out I don't belong here?"

Here's the thing that blew my mind: It's never about the actual business stuff. Nobody's lying awake at 3:00 a.m., worried about market analysis or competitive positioning. They're worried about whether they belong in the room at all. It's all imposter syndrome masquerading as business strategy.

I get why it's happening. We're living in a highlight reel where everyone's social media looks like they're crushing it 24/7. Meanwhile, you're over here like, *Did I just suggest something completely stupid in that meeting?* Spoiler alert: You probably didn't, but social media has us all convinced everyone else has their shit figured out while we're just winging it.

Here's what this fear epidemic is costing us: How many breakthrough ideas die in someone's head because they're thinking, *Who am I to suggest this?* Your brightest people are sitting on their best ideas, paralyzed by the fear of looking stupid. To make matters worse, the higher people climb, the more they have to lose. So they default to safe, conventional thinking.

The result? Organizations are full of incredibly capable people producing mediocre results because everyone's too scared to access their breakthrough thinking for fear of looking foolish.

While most people think that being fearless is to be "without fear," I'll argue that while that might be the literal definition, that's just ridiculous. The point of Becoming Fearless is to acknowledge the fear you feel, but feel it *less*. Is there a truly evolutionary predator about to attack you? Then, hell yes, fear is going to do some amazing things to help keep you alive. But most of us don't feel fear like that because we are trapped inside all day long. We've replaced the evolutionary reason to feel fear into anxiety over missed emails, passive-aggressive bosses, demanding clients, AI replacing jobs, potential layoffs . . . you name it, until we become scared of anything and everything that could spell change. But we must get back to a place where we have a healthy (a.k.a. biological) relationship with fear, and not the kind that keeps us trapped inside boxes.

The definition of fear is "an unpleasant emotion caused by the belief that someone or something is dangerous, likely to cause pain, or a threat." It's not entirely a bad thing. It has served us well throughout humanity's existence as we ran from saber-toothed tigers or avoided crossing raging rivers. But in today's modern age, fear presents itself like its "caveman state," but with the same acute response to things like, "My boss didn't approve my travel request, maybe I'm getting fired." Almost getting eaten by a mountain lion as opposed to losing your job is not even remotely the same thing. But our human brains don't see much difference.

Our fight-or-flight kicks in, and then, before we have time to calm down our central nervous system, we slide into anxiety mode and start feeling paralyzed by the possibilities. While fear can be great to keep you alive, it's also a powerful trigger to stop you from experiencing true growth. So how do we know the difference?

Just Jump

Nature is an excellent reminder of what real fear *is* and what it isn't.

In May 2016, I traveled to Dominica with my MBA cohort to study business in a developing country. This tiny Caribbean island holds the world's largest concentration of active volcanoes, and the highlight of the trip was an all-day hike to the world's second-largest boiling lake, guided by a local named Marvin with a thick Dominican accent—one of the most laid-back humans I've ever met. I mean, the dude wore loafers on a trail that covered almost seven miles and 2,500 feet elevation gain. I was immediately in awe of Marvin.

The trail was less than 12 inches across in places, with steep drops and no guardrails. I found myself hanging onto roots, hoping the mud would hold, as I scaled down the mountainside. Every muscle in my body and every brain cell was focused purely on positioning my next step. I was experiencing being 100 percent truly, authentically present out of a sense of survival and self-preservation.

Towards the end of our adventure and eight hours of hiking, you develop what I call "jelly legs"—that's where you're so tired and delirious from walking all day that you start acting drunk, or at least your legs do, buckling randomly and tripping over roots and rocks.

At the end of the day, we finally reached the notorious Titou Gorge, the famous gorge from *Pirates of the Caribbean* that Johnny Depp careens over to escape a tribe of cannibals who presumably want to eat him. Now that's real fear. Marvin turned to the group and asked, "Who wants to jump into the gorge?"

I knew I wanted to and stepped forward. As I looked around, I was standing alone. Everyone else was shaking their heads, except for my MBA professor, Ray Lamorgese. He just walked up to the cliff and jumped right in (after all, it wasn't his first time to the island).

Which left me standing about 30 to 40 feet above the water. Looking at the steep rock cliffs, which were only 10 feet wide on either side, I realized that if I didn't aim perfectly and keep my limbs tight to my body, I was dead. What was initially excitement turned into pure fear, and I became frozen at the edge.

> **"Don't think too much . . . otherwise you're not going to do it. Just jump."**

I'll never forget what Marvin said to me that day. It was the simplest advice:

"Don't think too much . . . otherwise you're not going to do it. Just jump."

I took the plunge. And never felt so alive.

Nature is the great equalizer; it reminds us of what real fear is and it challenges us to push past our own capabilities, physically and mentally, to understand what we are truly capable of.

Lost in the Desert

In 2024, I co-hosted a retreat in Sedona for women and created an epic experience to hike every day following a three-day plan of heal, discover, become. This was paired with a vortex hike and the right energy to match the focus of the day.

On the final day I had to pivot my hike plan last minute. A request around the campfire the night before from one of the retreat guests was to pick something "a little less strenuous." I always scout out hikes beforehand, but none in my back pocket fit the bill.

The next day, trying to wrangle an excited group eager to hit multiple trails, I took a wrong turn. We ended up on a much longer route, which was way more than most of the group had bargained for—over four miles and 500 feet of elevation gain in the Arizona desert. Mid-hike, at least half of the group were hot, sweaty, and miserable. I felt terrible. As we finished the hike, we were famished and grateful to be headed back to the house as the heat kicked up.

But something magical happened during testimonials the next day. Yes, the hike was too hard—but that wasn't the focus anymore. The focus was: "I can't believe I did it. It gave me confidence I didn't realize I had."

One of those women was Tracy Lube, who comes from a long corporate career in high-level sales operations and marketing roles at global insurance companies.

Tracy was sweating it out on that unexpected desert trek, but she wasn't just battling Arizona heat—she was wrestling with workplace demons. After years in high-pressure corporate roles at global insurance companies, she found herself trying to reinvent her identity with work while starting her own consulting firm. Tracy carried around a feeling many women in corporate America know. She shared with me that she was "overcoming the fear that I had of potentially losing my job, being belittled by men, and not being recognized for the true value that I brought to the table."

The pattern was exhausting. "We so often tend to shy away from those challenges that we think we can't do, especially as women," Tracy said. "We also shy away and defer rights to our male counterparts."

Tracy had become a master of saying yes to everything, working 80- to 100-hour weeks, because boundaries felt too risky. "I don't think people set enough boundaries with work because of their fear," she said. "They think they're going to get fired."

But something shifted on that dusty trail. "I did think at one point I was going to die from hypoglycemia," she laughs. Ironically, her blood pressure dropped from 130/90 to 110/70 during the retreat. More importantly, facing that physical challenge broke something open: "After the hike, the largest difference was that I came out of it with confidence.

That confidence reminded me what I can do and what I can achieve, and to anyone that doubts it, I learned to have a 'fuck you attitude.' Everyone has an opinion, but I learned that the only one that really matters is me."

A year later, Tracy was featured on a magazine cover, was working to launch HerMeno℠, an employee benefit service to educate women about menopause, and had landed a position with one of the largest global manufacturing firms. Now, when people panic about deadlines, Tracy's response is direct: "When people get stressed over their workload, my response as a leader is to ask my staff, 'Is someone going die?'" She continues using nature walks for strategic thinking and getting grounded because "being out there, for me, opened up my confidence again."

The woman who once worked herself into the ground from fear now tells her team: "It's five o'clock. Go home." Sometimes the most fearless thing you can do is have healthy boundaries with your work.

Don't Look Back

Since jumping into the gorge with Marvin, I've been able to use fear strategically in my life and my work. Back in 2017, I got a call from my boss telling me that my position managing global accounts had just opened on the West Coast. As someone born and raised in Pennsylvania, and dealing with mostly national accounts at that time, I felt his next words were surreal: "Would you want to move out west and take on a global portfolio of some of the largest Fortune 10 companies in the world?"

I asked him to give me 24 hours to decide. Gone were the days of tediously creating pros and cons lists and exploring every possible best-case and worst-case scenario. That night when Steve came home from his day job, I asked him if he was up for an adventure. We chose to not think too much and just jump.

But all of this comes with some of the best life advice I've ever received. When I was debating whether to leave one job and go work for a competitor in this global role, my long-time mentor said to me: "Jess, whatever you decide, just make a decision and don't look back."

When you are faced with a decision, you are being *challenged to grow.*

Remember the three rules of *Becoming Fearless*:

1. **Just Jump.**

    Don't think too much; get your aim and jump. Try the crazy idea, pitch the revolutionary offer. Just go for it.

2. **Are you going to die?**

    Is the company going to go under? If not, embrace it as an opportunity for growth.

3. Don't look back.
Once you decide, fully commit to it and don't look back. Regret is the enemy of innovation.

The most important part of Becoming Fearless is learning how to find a healthy relationship with real, biological evolutionary fear again, and nature is the perfect catalyst—reminding us of who is boss. It's not deadlines, or clients, or micromanaging bosses. It's the clock. It's the time we have left on this rock before we die.

While writing this book, I attended a showing of the documentary *Out There: A National Parks Story* by filmmaker Brenden Hall. I assumed it would be all about the histories and stories of the national parks. But this movie had a profound effect on me.

It was a journey into what the director thought would be visiting as many parks as possible, and it turned into the most amazing collection of human stories of the people who live, work, and travel through our national parks. One of those people was a backpacker named Julia Michalski, and she shared why she chooses to backpack alone.

As a woman in the backcountry, I get asked a lot of questions, like: "How are you not afraid to hike alone?" "What about creeps in the woods?" "What about wild animals?"

Julia shared that the two things that scare her are bears and snakes. And I agree with her. Julia also acknowledged nothing about how being with a man might make her any "safer" from these things, which had me laughing because it's so true. But it was what she said next that brought a tear to my eye:

"Fear just shouldn't inhibit you from doing beautiful things."

There have been so many times *fear* has stopped me from doing beautiful things. But also times I remember it didn't, like jumping into Titou Gorge, or entrepreneurship, or deciding to take my clients hiking to unlock business strategy. I didn't think too much, I just jumped, and it's become one of the most beautiful parts of my life. And now, on the trail, I inspire others to do the same. So now it's your turn. Are you going to let fear inhibit you from having your life's greatest adventures?

10

Developing Radical Self-Awareness

Alone with Your Thoughts

Remember that study from the University of Michigan where participants opted to give themselves a mild electric shock rather than sit alone with their thoughts for 6 to 15 minutes? That's us on steroids in a modern age of constant connection. While studies show that American adults are spending more alone time than ever, they are not spending time without their technology.

The real question is: How many minutes per day do you spend alone with your thoughts? Not reading a book, not surfing the internet, not doom scrolling, and not half-listening to your spouse or partner. I mean no other people, no distractions, just you. I'll bet less than an hour. Actually, less than 15 minutes for most of us. I challenge you to try, this week, to just notice how often you don't do it—and that even when you try, how painfully uncomfortable it is.

Back to the problem that inspired this book: We have a serious disconnection problem from ourselves. So how do we fix it? First, let's understand why we would have resistance to fixing it in the first place. Because that's the real problem. For me, one of the first times I met my resistance happened somewhere deep in the Arizona desert.

The Dream on My Wall

In May of 2019, I was standing at the edge of the canyon deep in the Arizona desert, looking down and enjoying the last few moments of being weightless before I strapped on my pack. I was about to descend to the valley below to hike the next 16 miles to a place so magical most people would never see it.

About four years earlier, I had pinned up a magazine clipping of Havasu Falls to my home office whiteboard, along with my sales goals and other bucket list items. I had stumbled across this picture during a transformational shift in my life. I remember looking at the stunning red rocks framed by crystal blue water, the allure of tranquil beauty only nature can provide. It gave me a sense of peace and hope and courage I desperately needed.

Little did I know when I put that picture up that reaching this magical place would take winning a permit lottery system, months of training to prepare, and packing everything I'd need for the journey on my back. Also, I would be completely disconnected from technology. There's no Wi-Fi signal in the canyon, so to have this experience required five days of being fully disconnected.

I was feeling incredible at the top of that canyon that day—how I normally feel at the start of a hike. So I took a moment to savor the overlook, before strapping on a heavy 35-pound pack, and the journey that lay before me.

Being unplugged in nature teaches us to embrace Radical Self-Awareness. When you're unplugged, you're not worried about phone calls, emails, texts, or posting on Instagram. In fact, when your digital reality ceases to exist for a period of time, you're forced to actually just hang out with yourself. You are marinating in your own thoughts. You are at one with that inner part of you that needs to be seen, heard, and acknowledged to live life to its fullest.

You're also no longer experiencing what Dr. David Strayer calls "inattentional blindness," where you fail to see something in plain sight. You are finally seeing the world around you in all its glory. I like to think of this as *the limitless effect,* like that moment in the movie *Limitless*, when Bradley Cooper takes a miracle pill and suddenly sees everything with crystal clarity. The world sharpens. Possibility expands. Combine that with the power of your attentional network being in default mode and actually seeing the world around you? Limitless.

After years of staring at a torn-out page of *National Geographic* on my office wall, my bucket list dream of hiking to Havasu Falls was coming to life. But it didn't happen overnight.

The Permit and the Plan

I watched Steve pace back and forth in our kitchen on the phone with his cousin, Kevin. They were planning to get us a permit. To hike to Havasu Falls, you go through Supai Village, which is widely considered the most remote village in the continental United States. The only way in or out is by foot, by mule, or in rare cases of emergency—helicopter. This village and the waterfalls beyond are managed by the Havasupai people, a Native American tribe that has lived in the Grand Canyon for over 800 years.

Hikers and backpackers not fully committed to the sweat of packing in their own gear can, for a nominal fee, rent a donkey to carry their pack the 16 miles to the crystal-clear waterfall and campsite. This leaves them free to have a lovely walk in the desert and snap many Instagram-worthy photos.

We are not those people. I didn't just want to see the waterfall I had dreamed about for years; I wanted to commit to the journey it would take to get there. I wanted the experience, the sweat, the training, and the adventure.

We got the permit. That snapped me out of my daydream and into reality. We had made a pact with Kevin and a few of his friends that we would all pull together trying for the permit lottery system, and whoever got it would register for the rest of us. One of us got it, which meant we were about to embark on the journey of a lifetime.

Then it dawned on me. How the hell was I going to carry a pack filled with supplies, food, and everything else we'd need for the five-day journey? While generally healthy and someone who hiked regularly, I had never been backpacking before. But that wasn't what scared me. What scared me was that I had chronic back issues stemming from an old work injury and one too many car accidents where I was rear-ended, leaving me forever in a perpetual state of whiplash. Not one to let fear get in the way, I came up with a plan: We would train, filling our packs with weight, and hit the trails every weekend and sometimes on weekdays to cover a few miles and train our bodies to handle the journey. I also committed to a very serious personal trainer who worked with professional sports teams—after all, we did live in Portland. He had me do ridiculous exercises, including the time he tied bungee ropes to my shoulders, put the treadmill on the highest incline, and simulated backpacking with elevation gain of about 500 feet per mile. I was in pure hell.

This wasn't fun. This wasn't what I'd imagined. This was hard work, and not just the physical kind. Mentally I started second-guessing my dream, wondering if this beautiful picture in my mind was worth it. What if I slowed down the group? What if I couldn't carry my weight? What if I had to ask Steve to carry more than his fair share? The self-doubt crept in, and the thoughts were not kind. I started resenting my own body. How could it betray me? I started feeling guilty for going years without giving myself the tools to properly heal my back or really invest in strength training in the first place.

The Nature Guru

At some point during the training, I caught up with an acquaintance—someone I had met months earlier at a work event who had left an impression on me. Yancy Wright is the CEO and founder of Casa Alternavida, a wellness retreat in Puerto Rico, where he leads transformational experiences for leaders and their teams. While initially intrigued by his journey and his practices to get us all to chill out, I was most struck by Yancy's calm presence that felt otherworldly. I'll never forget being in the middle of a work offsite where we were solving problems, brainstorming about clients, and absorbing our new compensation model, and at the height of the normal work stress, in walked Yancy.

To be honest, I don't remember much about what he said or taught us, but his presence said it all. This dude was clearly on another level. He shared his personal journey of experiencing burnout in corporate America. As the sustainability director at Sellen Construction, one of the largest general contractors in Seattle, his clients were the same Fortune 100 giants I was working with, and we had more in common than I could've imagined.

Yancy was also part owner of the firm, working insane hours, until one day it all caught up with him. He shared with me his story: "I ended up in the ICU, and having the doctor hand me a sheet of paper, saying, 'Hey, we need you to sign here to not hold us liable, because we're going to shock your heart with a defibrillator and it may not restart.' So that was the big wake-up call for me, and at that point I knew I was stressed out and overwhelmed. But I didn't realize I was burned out."

After he got out of the hospital, Yancy realized he needed a serious timeout. He requested a sabbatical, which the company needed time to consider. His position and experience were just too valuable to the company to let him go off wandering around for a few months to find himself. But even in the darkest hours, sometimes the universe has a plan. Two days after his sabbatical request, Yancy found out he had won a ten-day kitesurfing trip to Los Roques, Venezuela, sponsored by Patagonia, GoPro, and Cabrinha Kites. The trip became an agreed-upon compromise between his need for a break to find some clarity and the company's need to keep Yancy around. Remembering how pivotal the trip was for him to reevaluate his life, he shared:

"That time in nature was so profound. I had time to solidify a vision of creating a place and space for people like me that are stressed out, overwhelmed, and disconnected from themselves and nature. This time on the catamaran locked that in. I felt so connected to my essence, waking up with the sun and going to sleep with the moon rising. It was a necessary thing to help me reset, and motivate me to create my vision—something different but much needed."

After returning to work, Yancy made the radical decision to leave it all behind to start a leadership retreat in Puerto Rico. Now an executive coach and workshop facilitator, he helps people embrace the power of nature to chill the hell out and find clarity in their lives. Obviously, I was captivated by his story. When I asked him later about how this all came about, Yancy said, "When I was centered, when I was taking time for myself to be in nature and to just be curious, then openings would happen."

The Weight in Your Pack

Somewhere in the middle of training for Havasu, I reached out to Yancy for help with connecting the dots on one of my major accounts, as he still had a lot of great contacts in the Seattle area. But what I got was so much more than that. I remember telling him about preparing for my journey to Havasu Falls and my fear of my back holding me back, literally. I'll never forget what he said:

"I wouldn't be surprised if, once you got out there in nature, your back pain disappeared."

He went on to explain to me that the back represents a somatic principle.

"If emotions are energy in motion, then what emotions are you not expressing that might be creating disease in your body? Typically anger and frustration happens in the neck, jaw area, back of the neck, and shoulders. And the back, lower back, is carrying other people's stuff or the pressure that you're putting on yourself."

In that moment, I realized that, more than physical pain, my back issues represented all the weight I was carrying for others in the journey of life. I had no idea, but by jumping at the chance to climb to my own Havasu Falls, I had inadvertently started a journey to release decades of generational trauma and codependency issues, and essentially carrying other people's weight in my pack.

And it wasn't as simple as taking it off. Every training "hike" had now become some subconscious exercise in learning what was my weight to carry and what had never been mine to begin with. What we forget is that our brains, our bodies, and our emotions are all tied together. Often this connection works so seamlessly that we forget to distinguish between what's a physical ailment and what's a manifestation of emotional trauma we've forgotten to release.

The closer I got to the trip, the more ruthless I became with the weight in my pack. I started carrying about 40 pounds, and each step with my pack on training hikes felt like torture. One night I got everything out of my pack and laid it all out in our kitchen. I grabbed my computer and started an Excel spreadsheet, beginning the meticulous task of jotting down each item, its weight, and what it was for, and when I got to the end, a total of the weight I was planning on carrying.

It quickly became apparent it was too much. I realized that some of the ridiculous comforts or fancy gear was just extra weight I didn't need. I didn't need pop-up bowls to eat my meals; we could pour boiling water into the pouch and eat it. I didn't need deodorant, because after a day of hiking 16 miles and no showers, nothing was going to help. I didn't need more than two pairs of clothes because, let's be real, this wasn't a fashion show.

It also left room for one thing that I didn't need but desperately wanted: a torn-up copy of Michael Singer's *Untethered Soul*. I wouldn't have my cell phone or any digital distractions, and I just really wanted to read this book on a hammock.

With my pack down to 32 pounds, occasionally crying on the trail as I trained, I started to feel lighter. Not just from shedding the physical weight, but from the newfound freedom of letting go of dead emotional weight.

For years, I had been telling myself I had a bad back. And that was a bold-faced lie. It was an excuse, a self-imposed handicap. If you remember, humans (myself included) are masters of deflection. It sounds a lot better to say, "I can't, I have a bad back," than "My back issues stem from not strength training to counteract weak muscles or learning how to let go of an overinflated sense of responsibility for other people's shit."

In this process of training, with Yancy's words echoing in my mind, I realized I did have an unhealthy relationship with carrying loads that weren't mine to begin with—family dynamics, old wounds, and an overcommitted sense of responsibility I'd developed at a young age after my father died. I needed to learn how to choose which weight was mine to carry and which weight was holding me down with other people's stuff that I had to let go.

It hurts, it's painful, it's brutal and ruthless—and absolutely necessary—to live the life you were meant to live. Because the truth is, most of us go through life carrying weight that isn't truly ours, and until we heal and choose to let it go, it will keep weighing us down and keep us from ever reaching our own Havasu Falls.

Reaching Havasu Falls

Something surprising happened as I trained to hike to a dreamy waterfall—something I never anticipated. I started the journey to heal my back pain and, more importantly, the relationship I have with my body.

The journey to Havasu wasn't so much about reaching a beautiful waterfall as it was about finding myself again in a way only nature could provide. When we strip away all the distractions, the noise, and the other people and choose to walk a long while in the desert, we commit to finding a part of ourselves that's been buried for a long, long time.

Backpacking in nature, in movement, and unplugging, taught me the concept of Radical Self-Awareness and of stripping away the lies we tell ourselves: "We can't," "We won't," "It's too hard"—to the reality underneath. What we are avoiding is the thing that is most critical to our survival—not in a literal sense, because I had survived for years with a "bad back"—but in the spiritual sense that kept me from living a life where I felt truly *alive*.

While we are all hip to the concept of self-awareness—the ability to consciously know and understand ourselves, our emotions, and our thoughts and behaviors, both how they affect us and the people around us—Radical Self-Awareness is something much deeper.

Radical Self-Awareness forces us to slow down, breathe deeply, and understand who we truly are when no one is looking, without judgment. It's the unapologetic practice of seeing yourself clearly, sometimes for the first time. It's seeing your patterns, emotions, thoughts, strengths, and weaknesses, and understanding your blind spots and your impact, without judgment, distraction, or delusion. It is seeing *you* clearly—the good, the bad, the ugly, and the amazing all at once, without trying to fix it.

At some point, I found myself lying in my hammock in the campsite by Havasu Falls, *Untethered Soul* in one hand, swinging with the gentle breeze. Ironically, I was already learning the lesson in this book through my own lived experience—that I am not my thoughts or emotions, but the awareness observing them. I couldn't focus on the book, really. I put it down and, for the first time in a long time,

> **Radical Self-Awareness forces us to slow down, breathe deeply, and understand who we truly are when no one is looking, without judgment.**

I chose to just hang out with myself. I felt that my need to pack a book, however brilliant it was, was second to my need to just rock back and forth with my thoughts, watching them come and go without getting swept away. An overwhelming emotion of gratitude passed over me. I cried. I released the journey I had been on, thanked myself for being strong enough to let it all go, and let nature heal me in a way that only it can.

When I interviewed Yancy for this book, he reminded me of how powerful it can be to put yourself in nature's embrace. "I consider nature to be my therapist, to be my ally, to be my coworker, to be my guru, or mentor," he said. "Nature is all of the above."

If you sit back and get Radically Self-Aware, it's not enough to understand that you micromanage your team, are terrified of looking foolish, or play it safe when it comes to bold decisions for your company. Radical Self-Awareness forces you to peel back the layers and understand the *why* behind the what. But instead of jumping to judgement to fix it, just hang out with your own consciousness for a while. Because it might lead you to an understanding deep down inside. Only then can real change emerge.

Once we strip away the noise, the busyness of everyday life, and the—often inaccurate—stories we tell ourselves, we can see the world more clearly, as well as ourselves.

The point of developing Radical Self-Awareness is for you to reconnect with who you really are, because only then can you show up being Powerfully Present in your life and work.

11

Cultivating Powerful Presence

CEOs and Christmas

In that moment, I knew I had to do something, but felt confused and afraid to speak up. The meeting was going downhill, and not in a good way. I was sitting in a conference room with the global real estate team of one of the largest companies in the world. While I've had decades of high-level sales experience and knew how to read people and run a room, I wasn't alone. The CEO of my company was along for the ride. This opportunity was too big; the customer was too important, so of course he invited himself to the party.

As regional vice president of Global Accounts, it was my job to create the strategy for how to partner with this company and elevate the relationship beyond being just a vendor. I had to create strategic alignment around sustainability or innovation, or business practices—and I finally had all the right people in the room. Except there was one problem: I had lost control of the meeting the second my CEO said, "I think we should show them our latest sustainability video."

Cue my brain deflating. I knew this was the wrong way to spend the few precious minutes with my top customer while trying to have a positive impact and kick off our partnership. However, I wasn't in charge anymore.

Their real estate team presented their upcoming plans for global expansion, which was a great chance to engage and ask questions. But when they finally took their seat, my CEO cued up a promotional video. I watched in silent horror as confused looks went around the table. I could read their thoughts: *Is he really showing us a video right now? Is this guy serious?* And the tells were all too real. Just like at a poker table, people started fidgeting; some checked their phones or smartwatches. The head of global real estate seemed genuinely displeased and ready to bail.

As the promo video got to the end, I realized I had a choice: save the meeting and risk my job, or let the C Suite team from my company continue to make this a giant waste of everyone's time, leaving my job intact but also leaving a lasting impression on the customer that we've royally wasted their time. I took a deep breath and thought about my options. I had spent over six months planning this meeting and getting all the right people in the room. This moment was too important to just throw away. I swallowed my fear and checked my self-awareness. I was anxious, but so was the rest of the room.

I needed to do something, and *fast*. We only had a few minutes left. I watched my CEO like a hawk, waiting for the briefest pause in his diatribe, and just as he needed to pause, I took my chance. I jumped in and said, "We want to thank you for your years of business with us. The reason we asked for this meeting was to understand how we can become better strategic partners for you."

Then I channeled a great line from an old mentor of mine who taught me strategy: "Pretend it's Christmas. . . ."

That snapped everyone to attention. I could see them thinking, *Did she just say "Christmas?"* Yes, yes, I did. So I got their attention. Because no one says "Christmas" in a high-level business meeting, but now they were ready to hear what was next.

"Pretend it's Christmas," I said. "What's one thing we can do for you that has nothing to do with selling you flooring and everything to do with solving a business challenge?"

The woman who was the right hand of the head of global real estate said, "I'm so glad you asked. I have an idea."

And that five-minute conversation changed the whole trajectory of the meeting, the partnership with that client, and the next few years of revenue with our company. It all started with one tiny moment of Becoming Fearless, a dash of Radical Self-Awareness, and finding my own Powerful Presence in a room of titles more important than mine.

Finding Yourself in the Wild

The first time I truly understood Powerful Presence, I wasn't even trying to find it for myself. I was trying to find some sanity, or maybe clarity. Probably both. The three times in my life when I became seriously disconnected from myself had all pushed me into nature for some unknown reason, and it was there that I started to remember who I was, what I wanted to be, and how to show up as that person in my life and my work.

From Ridley Creek State Park in Pennsylvania, to Forest Park in Portland, to the foothills in Boise, one thing remained consistent—each time I committed to just showing up in nature, in movement, and leaving my technology behind, I found myself again. That's Powerful Presence. So few people have it in our modern society that it becomes a superpower to develop it. Powerful Presence is a superpower in leadership, in sales, in building a business, in being a parent, a spouse, and a friend. Why? Because we are all so distracted that being present in the moment feels almost unnatural. But it gives you a crazy competitive advantage in every interaction you have, because you show up as a real human again.

If you've ever walked into a room and met a person who locked eyes with you, asked thoughtful questions, and listened without waiting for their chance to interrupt—and maybe you felt a little "off" because they were so dialed in—that's Powerful Presence. It has nothing to do with titles, experience, money, or personality and everything to do with mastering all the other concepts in this book.

But what is Powerful Presence? First, let's talk about what it's not: It's not taking a walk while listening to a podcast. It's not answering emails while playing with your children. It's not having dinner with someone you love, just waiting for your phone to distract you. It's not being checked out in a high-level business meeting, just waiting for the clock to run out.

Powerful Presence is showing up as your authentic self, fully engaged and content to be exactly where you are in that moment in time.

Powerful Presence is showing up as your authentic self, fully engaged and content to be exactly where you are in that moment in time.

The best way to cultivate it is by going for a walk in nature, alone with your thoughts. And it's not easy. There are some uncomfortable moments in the beginning as we learn to be alone with ourselves again. But the payoff is worth it. Because when you choose to show up being Powerfully Present in your own life, the world opens up in unimaginable ways.

All of those moments hiking alone taught me something I'd been searching for my entire career: Powerful Presence isn't something you perform or achieve—it's something you remember. And the only way I knew how to help others remember was to take them where I had found it myself.

That's how Hike to Become Experiences were born. Not as corporate team building or outdoor adventure, but as something much simpler and more radical: a chance to remember who you truly are, why you're here on this planet, and how to show up as that leader in your life and your work again.

The format is straightforward because the magic isn't in its complexity. We start with what I call a "campfire chat"—not a traditional keynote, but an honest, story-driven conversation around a real fire that invites teams to let go of the noise and get grounded again. Then we head into the wild—forest, desert, mountain, or beach—it doesn't matter as long as it's in nature. What matters is removing the distraction of technology, getting in movement, immersing ourselves in nature, and being human again. It's really hard to explain to people who aren't ready to take a walk outside the box.

One early morning at 6:30 a.m., I led a hike for conference attendees—some of whom I had recruited the night before at the hotel bar. The goal? Help people gear up for a long travel day home. As with most of my morning hikes, turnout was modest. And on this particular day, it was the first morning of daylight savings time in Fort Worth, Texas. I wasn't holding out much hope. But six people showed up.

One of them was Tom Roberts, a former corporate executive turned consultant and expat whisperer. The moment I saw him, disheveled hair and all, I knew it was going to be a walk to remember.

I'd gotten to know Tom earlier in the week. With experience managing a billion-dollar P&L and running operations in Japan for a large pharmaceutical company, he'd reached what many would consider the height of his "success." And yet, he told me:

"At the pinnacle of my career, making the most money I'd ever made, having the most perks I've ever had, at the highest level of ability to get things done, I was just super unhappy. I got blood pressure problems . . . I got anxiety. I was diagnosed with clinical depression. I was the fish flopping around on the shore."

Eventually, he walked away from corporate life to start Cranberry Leadership. That's when our paths crossed.

That morning, Tom showed up begrudgingly and told me he was there more to support me than to hike. He even affectionately named our small crew "Better Friends Than Jess Deserves."

But something shifted during that walk. A tired, somewhat grumpy group shifted into smiles and laughter. When I asked Tom about the change, he said:

"I felt fantastic when I got finished with it. . . . Your brain is energized in a little bit different way. I'd gotten up, seen people I really had started to adore very quickly, and it was just great. I felt like the energy surge I had about midway through that walk carried through a long time."

Later that year, Tom became the first person to take the Hike to Become Challenge overseas, practicing the method while working in Japan. He believed in it so much, he introduced me to his former colleague, Kimberly Moran.

The Waterfall Moment

When I first met Kimberly Moran over Zoom, the words "delightfully warm" came to mind. For a woman in executive leadership at one of the biggest medical companies in America, who holds both a PhD and an MBA, delightfully warm wasn't what I was expecting. She made me miss corporate America and being part of a global organization when she described her team as the "Navy SEALs" of the company. This wasn't a business strategy for her—it was taking care of her incredible team members who had been under tremendous pressure to launch not one but two drugs that year. After meeting her, I wanted to create a memorable experience for all of them.

We started with a campfire chat around a real fire. After I shared my Hike to Become story, we talked about bucket lists, being fearless, and creating sacred time to be more Powerfully Present in our life and our work. We laughed, drank wine, and roasted marshmallows. The next morning, when we met at 7:00 a.m. for a hike in the beautiful Pacific Northwest, most people had already left their tech in the car. We started hiking . . . then came around the corner to see the waterfall, and I looked back. What I saw was amazing—no one was fumbling for their phone to document this moment. Everyone just stood there in awe, experiencing it.

Once we reached the waterfall, I led them in a forest bathing exercise to just "be" Powerfully Present in their own bodies. I reminded them to use all of their five senses to take it in—the sights, the sounds, the smells—and to just exist without any judgement or thoughts.

I found a spot overlooking the waterfall where I could see everyone as they took time alone. I started to feel extreme gratitude and, if I'm being honest, a little emotional. Because staring at the waterfall also reminded me of how much my dad would've loved this, and there in that moment in the rainforest, surrounded by some incredible clients, I shed a tear, thinking of how proud he would be of what I'd created and the impact it was having on other people. Then I told myself to get my act together because I was working—and needed to be Powerfully Present for my clients.

When I asked Kim what her experience was like as both the leader of the team and a participant herself, she shared with me that she "saw Jeff Boutelle play like he was a four-year-old by the edge of the stream . . . you could see people connecting with memories for themselves. You could see people just finally settling in. You could see that they were breathing more deeply."

Kim was right. From my spot overlooking the waterfall, I remembered seeing exactly what she meant. Jason had gone for a cold plunge and seemed totally in his element. Johannes stood perfectly still on a rock closest to the waterfall, just taking it in. Kim had found her own quiet spot to meditate. Somewhere in the distance, Jeff was completely absorbed, exploring that nearby stream like he had all the time in the world.

What struck me wasn't just that they were relaxed. It was that no one was rushing or in work mode anymore. No one was checking the time or glancing around to see what others were doing. They were just . . . there. Being fully present in their own skin again.

The Ripple Effect

After every engagement, I invite teams to participate in the Hike to Become Challenge on their own to incorporate the experience into their everyday lives. Exactly 31 days later, I check in and host a team meeting to discuss their experiences of hiking alone—how it was challenging at times, but also the differences it made in their work. Sometimes I would receive a quick text from Kim with a picture of a park in DC or San Diego. It was amazing to see her fully embrace the experience. I always tell the team leader that they are the example of how to bring this into their lives and inspire others, and she embraced it wholeheartedly.

When I asked Kim what she discovered about herself during the Hike to Become Challenge—hiking alone, unplugged, for 30 minutes every day for a month—her insights revealed the personal foundation that makes Powerful Presence possible.

"I need that alone time," she said. "It helps me think better. I can often resolve complex problems more. It's also important for me to role model it with my family."

She discovered something many leaders struggle to admit: "I am able to listen better and to be more focused on my employees. A lot of times, I have more of an expediency bias and get stuff done, and I'm able to pull myself back and read and listen to the room more, when I have that space."

This is the compound effect of Powerful Presence—it transforms how you show up everywhere. The experience created what Kim calls a "common language" for resilience and problem-solving.

But here's what the research doesn't capture about that 50 percent boost in problem-solving after nature immersion: It's not just cognitive. It's emotional. It's spiritual. When you strip away the noise and remember how to be present with yourself, you show up differently for everything else.

That moment was so profound for Jeff that he used his picture by the waterfall as his family Christmas card that year. As Kim told me months later, "I knew I had made an impact on him with that."

The Business Impact Nobody Talks About

This isn't just team bonding, it's a systematic approach to maintaining peak performance. As Kim calculates the return on investment (ROI): "If I could just have one of those leaders be a better leader that is more resilient and able to save just one resignation from, let's say, a salesperson, that's hundreds of thousands of dollars . . . you're looking at a hundred-fold X ROI."

The most powerful aspect of cultivating presence is how it spreads. Teams that have experienced this transformation start creating their own rituals. As Kim shared, "We went out for walks together from time to time. Even in my one-on-ones with my direct reports that went through the experience, I'm like, 'Have you been outside lately?' It's a great reminder of us as a tool for resilience."

Kim embraced this practice so fully as a leader. "You have to put yourself first. It's the oxygen mask on the plane. If you don't put your oxygen mask on, you can't help others. So if you are not at your best [in] your ability to lead your team, you're telling yourself a lie."

One of the people who went through this experience had some pretty significant life events that happened afterward. Kim believed it was "because we now have this common language about going outside, taking a pause, seeing some trees, breathing in the air, and disconnecting. That helped that person get through some really hard things in life, and that, to me, you can't put an ROI on."

After the first Hike to Become Experience, John Finch, CEO and president of Legacy Group, was inspired to take his partnership team on a hike before their meeting. When I asked him what happened next, he said, "We actually had some tougher conversations after the hike. But the hike really greased the skids because people felt more connected and braver to bring up subjects that were on their mind. It worked out perfectly."

Where Presence Lives

The shocking reality is that, regardless of where or how we work, most of us have no idea how little we are showing up in our life and our work. We are too busy to stand still. Society tells us that, unless we are in an office or tethered to technology, we are not "working" or being "productive." But I've actually found that the opposite is true.

That moment in the conference room taught me that Powerful Presence isn't about titles, experience, or affluence. It's about being so grounded in who you are and what matters that you can think clearly and act decisively when everyone else has lost the plot. And the only way I learned to access that level of presence was by spending time alone on the trail.

When you're walking in the woods without distractions, you're committed to being present with yourself. This is an incredible skill to learn, to cultivate, and to pull into your everyday life. Powerful Presence means being so calm and at ease within yourself and your surroundings that you are the rock that the waves crash against or the tree that the wind whips through, but nothing can phase you. And like this rock or this tree, you have dealt with your emotions, have calmed yourself, and are ready for any situation, whether it's scaling a mountain, undertaking a challenging hike, or having a difficult business meeting with a client.

Whether you're leading a Fortune 500 company or building a startup, the principles remain the same. Powerful Presence starts with creating space—space to think, space to feel, space to simply be human in a world that profits from your distraction.

The trail teaches us that being present isn't a luxury; it's a requirement for accessing our best thinking, our deepest creativity, and our most authentic leadership. When you show up being Powerfully Present, you give others permission to do the same.

The Hike to Become Challenge reminds us that this work starts with us, by developing Powerful Presence alone with ourselves on the trail. Because until you learn how to be Powerfully Present for yourself, you cannot show up for anyone else.

12

The Wild Advantage

What's Yours?

When you pick up a book with the subtitle *Why Your Brain on Nature Is Your Boldest Business Move*, you're probably expecting some secret recipe to unlock innovative thinking. What you might not have anticipated is that it takes a journey to get there. The 31-day hike challenge of Climbing The Mountain in Your Mind to Become Fearless, develop Radical Self-Awareness, and cultivate Powerful Presence all leads to reaching your strategic summit.

At your strategic summit, you discover the three things most people don't know—who you are, what you were put on this planet to do, and how to show up as that person in your life and work.

This is where you find your Wild Advantage.

What is your Wild Advantage?

Your Wild Advantage is the crazy business and leadership approach only you can do because it's authentically you.

It's not what business school taught you. It's not in industry "best practice" reports. It's the unconventional method that emerges when you stop trying to fit into someone else's definition of professional success and start building from who you truly are.

> **Your Wild Advantage is the crazy business and leadership approach only you can do because it's authentically you.**

And here's the thing: From a business strategy standpoint, it should seem crazy to everyone else. That's exactly why it works.

When Starbucks CEO Howard Schultz decided to transform coffee shops into a "third place"—not home, not work, but somewhere in between—based on the concept originally developed by sociologist Ray Oldenburg, critics rolled their eyes.

Who would pay a few dollars for coffee and then hang out for hours? Turns out, millions of people would. It redefined retail space and reshaped global café culture. At the time, Americans bought a $1 cup of coffee at a gas station or a diner. Critics thought that the typical American was too fast-paced to sit down in an actual coffee shop like Europeans do. Investors were skeptical; they didn't see the business case for this wild idea to make money. Today, Starbucks is not known as a coffee shop, but as a *destination*. An experience. A place to have a casual business meeting or connect with friends.

When Ray Anderson, founder of Interface, declared his mission to run the world's first environmentally sustainable carpet company, people called him crazy. A carpet manufacturer cutting carbon emissions? It sounded like a terrible business idea. But he proved them wrong and made money doing it. Interface became the model for how purpose and profit not only coexist, but should be the new norm.

When Patagonia ran a full-page ad on Black Friday saying, "Don't Buy This Jacket," it wasn't a typo. It was a radical invitation to buy less, think more, and act consciously. It was a reminder of what Patagonia stands for: quality products that last forever with a positive environmental impact versus the looming black Friday hype that screams, "Buy more, buy now, consume!" And you know what? Sales soared, proving that honesty and values can outperform hype.

Some of the boldest business moves in history started as ideas that sounded borderline ridiculous:

- Phil Knight believed work should feel like play.
- Steve Jobs believed everyone should own a computer.

- Yvon Chouinard believed employees should be free to chase waves.
- And I believe we should take work for a hike to unlock our wildest ideas.

Each one was a Wild Advantage, a vision so personal and unconventional it made perfect sense to the person who said it and (almost) no one else. At first. But that's the thing about trailblazing ideas. They don't follow logic, they follow purpose. And eventually, the world catches up.

Finding your Wild Advantage requires a journey that can't happen behind a desk or when we're constantly distracted by technology. It demands stepping outside conventional approaches, trusting authentic instincts over proven formulas, and risking looking somewhat insane to discover what only you can do. So how do you know if it's crazy enough to succeed?

The Three Tests

Your Wild Advantage must pass three essential tests and the same principles we've explored throughout this journey:

1. Become Fearless: Is it crazy enough that no one else is doing it? Does it make traditional thinkers uncomfortable? Would most people in your industry consider it too risky?

2. Radical Self-Awareness: Is it core to who you are? If you couldn't make money doing this, would you still have a burning desire to pursue it? Does it emerge from your deepest values and natural inclinations?
3. Powerful Presence: Does this let you show up authentically in both life and work? Can you be truly yourself while implementing this approach? Do others experience the real you through this method?

All three must be present. Different isn't enough. You must be authentically different in a way that creates a genuine competitive advantage.

Trail Days and Monster Hikes

One of the things that intrigued me most about interviewing Ron Schneidermann wasn't just that he was the former CEO of AllTrails—it was that he recently stepped away from his high-growth career in tech and startups. Under his leadership, AllTrails expanded from a small team to over 200 employees, grew its user base to more than 60 million people worldwide, and was named one of the Best Apps of the Year in 2023 by Apple. The app now offers over 450,000 curated trail routes across 191 countries, solidifying its position as the world's largest and most trusted outdoor platform.

What I didn't expect was his down-to-earth yet boldly innovative approach to leadership. But it all made sense. Companies don't often grow by playing it "safe."

As CEO of AllTrails, Ron didn't just encourage outdoor time, he built it into the company's business model. The idea happened when his birthday fell on a Friday, and he decided he wanted to take the day off to go mountain biking. He brought some AllTrails colleagues along for the ride and found that the outing worked so well, he made it part of the company's culture.

Ron declared all employees should take a day and spend it on the same trails they developed the app for. Encouraging time spent in nature, in movement, and the whole plugged-in thing? Totally optional. What transpired wasn't just a day off playing hooky. It became AllTrails' innovation incubator. Trail Days became a companywide tradition that, on the first Friday of the month, all employees would get outside. The ask? Any wild ideas were captured afterward.

As Ron put it, "Trading one day a month behind the screen for so much positivity and impact was and is a no-brainer investment."

Trail Days became AllTrails' secret weapon, a dedicated time when the entire team disconnected from screens and reconnected with the trails their millions of users were exploring. By remembering the mission of the company and putting themselves in the place of their clients, team members started coming out with some great ideas.

"When we are chained behind our desk and chained behind our computer, it's tunnel vision," Ron explained. "But by creating space, you unlock creativity and innovation that just doesn't happen when you're focused on the day-to-day grind."

Ron estimates that 75 percent of AllTrails innovations resulted from Trail Day inspirations. One of the most important ideas, the AllTrails Apple Watch app, actually came from being outside, not staring at screens. Ironically, the team developed better technology simply by stepping away from it.

During our interview, one of my favorite topics was strategic planning in the wild. Ever since that fateful 31-day hiking challenge in January 2024, I've been taking business strategy on the trail with my clients, companies, and organizations to help them find clarity and unlock big ideas. And . . . so has AllTrails, led by Ron.

While other companies trap executives in sterile conference rooms, Ron's team headed to Yosemite and embarked on what he calls a "monster hike" before creating their strategic plan and tackling their biggest business challenges. Strategic planning in the wild works because, according to Ron, "It is the most productive and impactful day of the entire year."

Ron's instinctive approach validates what I've been experiencing with my clients: Strategic planning in nature isn't just more enjoyable, it is *way more effective*. When leaders discover this approach, they often ask me to facilitate their own wilderness strategy sessions, bringing my proven framework to their most critical business decisions. Because you don't have to be an outdoor company to experience business strategy in the wild.

Ron's approach, from starting Trail Days to unlock innovation to strategic planning in Yosemite, passes all three tests: (1) It was unconventional enough that competitors weren't doing it (Fearless); (2) it emerged from his authentic love of the outdoors (Radical Self-Awareness); and (3) it allowed him to lead this company from a place of authenticity (Powerful Presence).

This sounds inspiring coming from the former CEO of a tech company whose mission is to help the world find its way outside. But it can be easily done by almost everyone, because the reality is, we all can unlock our best ideas in nature. I've led strategic planning for a board of a Seattle non-profit where we spent the afternoon hiking in Discovery Park and reimagined their vision statement while staring at the Pacific Ocean. I've taken global executives forest bathing in the woods to find their own Powerful Presence.

Tom Roberts, the former corporate executive who'd shown up, hair disheveled, to that 6:30 a.m. hike and dubbed our small crew "Better Friends Than Jess Deserves," captured something essential about the work I do when I asked him to explain what had shifted during our hike together:

"What you do when you're out there is create space for magic to happen. We never focus on creating space for magic. We focus on 'Let's just work our asses off and hope the magic happens.' But you're taking a proactive approach to create space for whatever that magic is to happen. We need more magic."

Tom believed so much in my work that he referred me to Kimberly Moran and her team, which led to our epic forest bathing by the waterfall experience. Once Kim experienced it for herself, she was able to articulate what I do in a way that most others have to experience it to understand:

"We are out here paying expensive consultants to tell us what to do. When, what if we have the answers inside of us all along? All we have to do is access them. That's what you show people—you guide them into the answers they already have."

The transformation extended beyond her immediate team. "We took new ideas," Kim said. "'What if we did this with the team? What if we did that?' We were able to think about the experience we went through to make our teams better—changing meeting formats, being clearer on strategic initiatives."

Kim's measurable results represent what's possible when we step away from the noise and tap into the answers inside of us. When we choose to be Powerfully Present over chronically busy and when we show up to work with some Radical Self-Awareness, wild ideas just appear.

After people kept referring to me as "the hiking girl" or "business strategist in boots," I decided to give myself a new title. What started out as a joke, referring to myself as a "Chief Hiking Officer," suddenly became my calling card. When you think about it, it makes sense. Because the number one job of a CEO is creating the strategic vision for the company. Most of my work is some form of business strategy; I've just found a better environment for unlocking wild ideas than in a boardroom.

At the trailhead, I show up like a cool aunt who steals cell phones. Then I remind people to stop worrying about step counts and breathe in the terpenes. Once we've hit all the markers, I need for their brains to turn on, I ask the right questions to unlock wild ideas. That's where the magic happens.

Building a Wild Advantage Culture

The most innovative companies aren't arguing about old problems, like hours spent in the office or return-to-work policies. They are shifting the conversation away from the convention of boxes and into a new territory—redefining the way we work. Here's how to start making that shift in your own workplace, on your team, and even into your life if you work remotely.

Step 1: Bring the Hike to Become Challenge into your workplace.

> Everyone should get one innovation meeting every day: in nature, in movement, unplugged, for at least 30 minutes. Watch your creativity skyrocket.

Step 2: Ditch the office myths.

> Make it clear with new work policies that you believe the best ideas can happen outside of the conventional "in office," "behind a desk," and "tethered to tech" unspoken rules, and then create space for it to happen. Start with the leadership team and watch the company transform.

Step 3: Create company traditions, outside.

> Culture isn't created in a quarterly all-hands meeting; it's built in the spaces in between. Find ways to create your own company traditions that require time outside, in movement, and unplugged. Just be ready to capture the brilliant ideas that happen.

> Love rafting? Make it your annual pre-strategy ritual.
>
> Product launch coming up? Take the design team on the trail.
>
> Want to ward off burnout? Let your people go surfing—literally.

Step 4: Bring in an expert.

> Some companies arrive at outdoor innovation by accident. Often, people are inspired by the guides who have forged a path ahead of us. My path wouldn't be the same if it hadn't been for some of the trail guides who came before me. Choose which destination feels right for you and your team.

As the Chief Hiking Officer and founder of Hike to Become, I guide leaders and teams through an actual method designed to use nature, movement, and unplugging to solve business challenges and spark innovative ideas. I have taken executive teams into the outdoors to align strategy, improve team dynamics, and uncover wild ideas that would not surface in the four walls of a conference room.

My Wild Advantage Discovery

My Wild Advantage discovery happened on a freezing foothill outside Boise, somewhere between days 15 and 21 of my hiking challenge. I was questioning everything about my traditional consulting business when the realization hit: *If hiking unlocks my best ideas, why don't I take clients hiking?*

It felt completely crazy. Who asks corporate executives to strap on hiking boots in the middle of a keynote presentation? Who builds a business model around something as "unprofessional" as walking in the woods? Who challenges the idea that muddy boots are bad for business?

If you remember Dr. David Strayer's observation of inattentional blindness—the idea that we don't see at least 50 percent of what is right in front of us because we are too distracted—the same principle applies to business strategy. We often don't see the most obvious answers right in front of our faces.

Every wild business idea in this book proves that being in nature, in movement, and unplugged can unlock breakthrough ideas. We've just forgotten how to do it and why it matters.

The difference between legends like Phil Knight, Steve Jobs, and Yvon Chouinard—and the rest of us—isn't talent or luck. It's the unrelenting courage to trust what feels authentically right, even when it contradicts conventional wisdom.

My Wild Advantage passes all three tests:

1. Become Fearless: No one else was systematically taking executives hiking and using science-based metrics to unlock strategic insights. It seemed crazy enough that most consultants would never risk their reputation on such an unconventional approach.
2. Radical Self-Awareness: Even if I couldn't make money from it, I'd still be drawn to helping people think more clearly outdoors. It combines everything core to who I am—my love of nature, my analytical mind, and my passion for unlocking human potential.
3. Powerful Presence: Leading hikes allows me to be authentically myself—outdoorsy and strategic, scientific and intuitive, professional and playful. I don't have to choose between my fierce love of the outdoors and business expertise; they actually amplify each other.

The results transformed everything. John Finch, CEO of The Legacy Group, became the first leader brave enough to say yes to my unconventional keynote format. His immediate response launched what would become Hike to Become: "I believed in what you were putting out there. It was simple for me."

Within two years, my business revenue tripled. I was chosen as a TEDx speaker to share my message of "Why We Are Afraid to Walk into the Woods." That same week, I was asked to challenge workplace norms at DisruptHR with my talk "How Nature Fuels the Future of Work." This book exists because I trusted an idea that felt authentically mine, even when it seemed a little too crazy to everyone else.

But the real Wild Advantage isn't found in just financial success, writing a book, or speaking on global stages. It is alignment between who I am and how I work. My authentic desire to work outside, combined with my data-driven approach to strategic thinking, created something no competitor could replicate. That's because it emerged from my unique journey, my business expertise, and my authentic desire to work—outside.

The Future of Work Is in the Wild

Today, executives from Fortune 500 companies to innovative startups are remembering what we've known all along: Our human brains work best in nature, in movement, and unplugged from technology. They've discovered what John Finch and Kimberly Moran learned—sometimes the most innovative thing you can do is step outside, literally and figuratively, and trust what emerges when you create space for your authentic self to show up.

But here's what I've learned, after guiding hundreds of leaders through this process: Knowing this intellectually and actually implementing it are two very different things. The gap between inspiration and transformation happens when you fully commit to stepping outside—in movement and unplugged.

Your breakthrough approach is waiting to be discovered, but it won't emerge from another strategy session in a conference room. It requires the courage to step away from what feels safe and productive—to do something that might look crazy to everyone else.

Ask yourself: *What unconventional approach keeps drawing my attention?* Because the universe is always sending us signs. What would you pursue even without financial incentive? How could you bring more of your authentic self to your professional work?

The leaders who are already practicing this don't wait for permission. They're the ones scheduling walking meetings instead of Zoom calls. They're building "Trail Days" into their company culture. They're taking their biggest strategic challenges outside and watching breakthrough solutions emerge. They understand that, in a world of artificial intelligence and automated everything, the most valuable competitive advantage is the magic of the human mind.

Your 31-Day Challenge Starts Now

If you've read this far, you already know something needs to shift. The question isn't whether nature-based thinking works—the research and stories in this book prove it does. The question is: What are you going to do about it?

Start tomorrow. Before you check email, before you dive into your calendar, step outside for 30 minutes. No agenda, no phone, no destination. Just walk and pay attention to what thoughts surface. Then do it again the next day. Do this for 31 days and document what happens. I guarantee you'll find clarity, develop Powerful Presence, and unlock wild ideas that would never happen in the box of the office.

Because here's the truth: Your competitors are still trapped in conference rooms, chasing best practices, and trying to innovate from behind screens. While they're stuck in conventional thinking, you could be discovering the one approach that makes you impossible to compete with.

At the intersection of Becoming Fearless, developing Radical Self-Awareness, and cultivating Powerful Presence is where your unique Wild Advantage lives. Whether you discover it through a highly curated experience like Hike to Become, or choose to forge your own path, the goal remains the same: the crazy business approach only you can do because it's authentically you.

This isn't just about personal fulfillment, your genuine approach to leadership, your unconventional solution to industry problems, your idea that could only come from you—it's about the impact you're meant to make and the people whose lives you will impact.

The world needs your Wild Advantage. And it needs it now.

The world needs your Wild Advantage. And it needs it now.

The only question left is: Are you fearless enough to step outside and find it?

Epilogue

There's No Wi-Fi in the Woods

There's a coffee shop mural I see every day that stops me cold: "There is no Wi-Fi in the forest, but you will find a better connection." I stare at it every time and think about just how different my life is, all because I went for a walk in the woods.

But that is just the start of the story. While I kept showing up to test my theory on the hiking trail and helping people find Powerful Presence and unlock wild ideas, the concept of writing a book—while raising toddlers and building a business—seemed about as likely as finding Sasquatch under my bed. Until I got a phone call from Monica Rothgery, former COO of KFC, US. We started a budding friendship a year earlier in a mastermind community, and I was drawn in by her corporate experience and direct style. She called to give me feedback on the TEDx, but had another idea in mind, asking, "When are you going to write your book?"

Monica has always told me how much my work and ideas have merit. As someone who has lived her life in corporate America, and the occasional hiker, she just "gets it." She pushed me when I had lost the will to push myself. For that, I'm eternally grateful.

In the journey to write this book, there have been so many moments of trail magic along the way. One of the people I interviewed for the book was Bruce Garthwaite, who has hiked parts of the Appalachian Trail. He told me about something thru-hikers call "trail magic" . . . when something serendipitous happens that cannot be explained, but it's like a guardian angel, God, the universe—maybe even nature herself—looking out for the brave souls who hike miles into the woods. It may be you have a busted-up foam pad and at the next lean-to, someone has left a brand new one behind. There's a beautiful, unspoken language of thru-hikers that feels like we are all intrinsically connected . . . hence, trail magic.

As I struggled to finish this book an idea occurred to me: Maybe I just needed to run away to a cabin in the woods and write. That first night, I didn't write a word, I just faceplanted into bed at 7:30 p.m. The next morning, I hit about 1,000 words. Then I decided to take a break for a hike and to eat some breakfast.

I remembered a former work colleague, Christopher had mentioned his childhood best friend owned a pastry shop in town. I reached out, and he made a text introduction. With a loose plan to swing by the bakery, Christian offered to give me a tour of his farm. As I waited, I started questioning why I was there. Frustrated, I felt like I was giving up on my writing goals to tour a farm, and thought, *What the hell am I doing? I should be writing.* Then I remembered to breathe. I remembered what my friend told me about trail magic, and of course reminded myself to practice being Powerfully Present. I don't believe in accidents; I believe in a universal plan, and there was a reason I was right there in that exact spot.

Christian radiates calmness and positivity. We walked around his property and, as we talked, he mentioned his full-time job managing a law firm. I was dumbfounded. In between running a farm, owning a bakery and managing a law office, how could he find the time? So I asked him, "Christian, do you even sleep?"

He laughed and said, "I do, actually, and quite well. I also find time to be with my family, which is what's most important. It's just when we are together, we're working on the farm, hiking, enjoying nature."

He asked what brought me to McCall, and I told him about writing this book. His eyes lit up and he said, "I'm not surprised. My best ideas always happen in nature."

There's a reason Christopher had reached out to me three weeks prior, after not speaking for years. A reason I was in a cabin in McCall, and a reason Christian wasn't traveling in Mexico. I asked him, "Can I interview you for the book?"

He said, "Sure!"

His story is now part of this book. Because . . . trail magic.

From meeting Ron Schneidermann to tracking down Dr. David Strayer, and all the brave voices and client stories in this book, I believe they are all here because—trail magic. None of this would've been possible if I hadn't chosen to disconnect from what doesn't matter to find a connection with what truly does.

A book that started out as "my story" quickly turned into "our story." As I set out to redefine the way we work, I found others along the path who were doing the same thing. As I was challenging the status quo, I realized I wasn't alone. On this journey to redefine the way we work and repair our relationship with nature, I found that we are ultimately finding a way back to . . . ourselves.

Our best, biggest, brightest ideas aren't waiting for us behind a screen or in back-to-back Zoom meetings. They live out there—where our brains can turn on, declutter the noise, and find peak performance. I want you to remember me freezing my

EPILOGUE: THERE'S NO WI-FI IN THE WOODS

ass off on top of a foothill in January, questioning my life decisions, and the moment I slipped in the mud and almost gave up.

Now, remember all of the incredible stories in this book:

- Rick, leaning against that tree on the Legacy Group hike, threatening to kill me if I took a picture—who went on to lose 15 pounds, cut sugar from his diet, and go on a dirt bike excursion with his grandkids without getting tired.
- Dakota, who had buried his idea to inspire the next generation of young men "deep in the basement" for a whole year—until a Hike to Become Experience and some wild prompts on the trail gave him the courage to speak his truth and start building his vision.
- Tracy, sweating it out in the Arizona desert, thinking she might die from hypoglycemia—who emerged with confidence and perspective. She launched HerMeno, landed a position with the largest global manufacturing firm, and now tells her team, "It's five o'clock. Go home."
- Kimberly's pharmaceutical team, launching two drugs for rare diseases under crushing pressure, who found their "common language" for resilience and faster strategic decision-making after their Hike to Become Experience where they stared

- at the waterfall in the Pacific Northwest rainforest.
- Zane, whose strategic planning session moved from a rainy conference room to the trail the following week—where we outlined not just his strategic business plan, but his entire intellectual property framework in half the time, with twice the clarity.

There are so many more crazy stories that, for one reason or another, did not make it into this book. Some people choose to keep their trail revelations a secret, and as their guide, I always honor that request. But just know there are more wild ideas and inspired minds thanks to time spent on the trail with Hike to Become.

Now imagine the impact you can have. There must be something that seems crazy, maybe even a little impossible, in the back of your mind. Just like the concept of trail magic, I believe you picked up this book for a reason. But what you do next determines the ripple effect you can have.

None of these transformations would've been possible had I given up or listened to that voice that told me it was too crazy. None of this would be possible if I hadn't chosen to disconnect from what doesn't matter to find a connection with what truly does. It helps that there is no Wi-Fi in the woods.

At the beginning of the book, I reminded you of what's at stake if we don't heed the call. We are in a battle for our humanity. Technology is a wonderful tool, but it's time we remind it—and ourselves—that it is just a tool. We are the creators of our own destiny. Humans are brilliant; we just need to make the time to remember it, and step into the perfect environment to stop the noise and unlock innovative ideas.

This book isn't *just a book*—it's a sign. A call to action. A quiet whisper to put on your hiking boots, or running sneakers, or beat-up loafers. If you want to unlock your wildest ideas, change your company, and help me inspire a movement, you'd better get ready. That's why you picked up this book.

So I have one question for you . . .

What are you waiting for?

Acknowledgments

Hiking Partners: Thank you to the brave souls who trusted me enough to leave their phones behind and follow me into the woods in search of their next breakthrough . . .

John Finch, for saying yes to my crazy idea and always being one of my biggest supporters. Tracy Lube, for following me into the desert and trusting me to share parts of your story. Kimberly Moran and Tom Roberts, for being such advocates for the work I do and opening your heart and mind to forest bathing and early morning hikes. Zane and Grayson Sterling, for trusting the method, embracing it wholly, and making me laugh along the way. Christan Toebe, for a river walk and talk, and sharing your story.

Trail Guides: Every great adventure needs expert guides who know the trail or have blazed their own. My thanks to . . .

Ron Schneidermann, for sharing your journey and insights with me. It made this book come alive. Dr. David Strayer, for picking up the phone and sharing your vast knowledge on how our brains behave in nature. I'm eternally grateful for the work that you do and someday hope to come join you. Yancy Wright, for inspiring me to see beyond my capabilities and unpack the weight in my metaphorical backpack. Gina Nelson, for trusting me to not get stuck in the mud and sharing your expertise. Marvin, for being the coolest trail guide in loafers and inspiring me to "just jump." Ray Lamorgese, for jumping before me and never doubting my crazy ideas.

To my cousin Eric, who thru-hiked the Appalachian Trail when I was a kid and inspired me to believe that anything is possible if you go for a long walk in the woods.

Base Camp Support: No one makes it to the summit alone. Thanks to . . .

Steve, my trail partner and the supporter of all my craziest dreams. None of this is possible without you. Thank you for always having my back, pushing me out the door to hike on hard days, and reminding me of why it's all worth it. Brynn, my little hike leader. Your joy for the trail and enthusiasm for Hike to Become makes me smile. Someday you'll run the company. Tristan, for reminding me to be Powerfully Present when I forget. My mom and dad, for instilling in me a love of nature and a heart to help people. My grandparents, who taught me the value of hard work and that anything is possible if you set your mind to it. Gavin—there aren't enough toasted sandwiches in the world to thank you for saving me from myself, from technology, and from ants after I hugged a tree.

My content editors and friends who dropped everything to read a manuscript and pushed me to share my message with the world: Andrew Hartman, Carson Green, Brad Root, Mike Pawlawski, Tom Roberts, Monica Rothgery, Tom DeAngelo, and all the members of the sidepieces for keeping me grounded through the process. And to Matt Todd, for your friendship and dancing on the trail.

Ignite press: To Everett, who saw the possibilities in this book before I could, and the team: Zelda and Malia. Thank you for helping me bring this adventure to life.

Help Me Start a *Wild* Movement (The Good Kind)

Hey friend,

You made it. Through the stories, the science, the soul-searching, and hopefully into the wild a little more often.

If this book made you laugh, rethink your relationship with your phone, or seriously consider hosting your next brainstorm session on a hiking trail . . . I have a favor to ask.

Leave a review. It's the best way to help other burned-out leaders and over-caffeinated executives find this book when they're staring at their computer screens, wondering how the hell to think clearly again.

Here's how:

 1. Go to the site where you bought the book.

2. Search for *The Wild Advantage* or my name.
3. Drop a few honest lines (doesn't need to be a novel).
4. Bonus points: Post a photo with your copy in the wild. Desk shots are fine. Tree shots are better.

And if this book sparked something big? Share it.

- Gift it to your favorite "Why are we still in this meeting?" coworker.
- Drop it on your boss's desk before the next company retreat.
- Start a movement at work—the good kind.

You can help me get more people off autopilot and into the wild, where they can think like humans again. Imagine the magic we can make . . .

Thank you for hiking this journey with me. Our adventure is just about to begin.

Stay Wild,

Jess

Want the Author to Come Speak to Your Organization?

Here's how to hit the trails with Hike to Become:

Jessica DeAngelo speaks to teams, takes strategy on the trail, and helps executives trade burnout for breakthrough ideas. She packs up her hiking boots for a limited number of speaking engagements and executive strategy sessions each year—preferably near trees, mountains, and trails.

Ready to explore?

Drop a line: jess@jessicadeangelo.com
Wander over: www.jessicadeangelo.com

Come with an open mind. Leave with a wild idea and maybe a few blisters.

Sources and Inspiration

For the curious readers, fact-checkers, and closet history buffs . . . here's where some of the bold claims and wild ideas came from.

Chapter 1: We Have a Connection Problem

Henry David Thoreau, *Walden; or, Life in the Woods* (Ticknor and Fields, 1854), 90. Classic text on deliberate living and connection to nature, source of the opening quote about living deliberately and learning what life has to teach.

Christian L. Lange, "Nobel Peace Prize Lecture," Speech, The Nobel Prize, December 13, 1921, https://www.nobelprize.org/prizes/peace/1921/lange/lecture/#:~:text=Technology%20is%20a%20useful%20servant,the%20state%20and%20to%20others. Early 20th-century perspective on technology as "useful servant but dangerous master," providing historical context for technology–human relationship concerns.

Frozen II. Directed by Chris Buck and Jennifer Lee (Walt Disney Pictures, 2019), 00:32:58. https://www.disneyplus.com/browse/entity-3f9272e2-33f1-47db-bb2e-9aa2c7c85a96. Source of Olaf's quote about technology being "both our savior and our doom," illustrating how even popular culture recognizes the double-edged nature of technological advancement.

Ron Schneidermann, interview by author, Zoom, May 2, 2025. Former CEO of AllTrails discussing the tension between technology and nature, describing the "existential battle versus screens" and advocating for outdoor time as a counter to digital addiction.

Kateryna Hanko, "35 + Must-Know Phone Usage Statistics for 2022," Clario, April 8, 2022, https://clario.co/blog/phone-usage-statistics/. Modern statistics on digital device usage patterns, including daily phone interactions and screen time data.

"Mobile touches: A study on humans and their tech," Dscout, June 15, 2016, https://pages.dscout.com/hubfs/downloads/dscout_mobile_touches_study_2016.pdf. Research study documenting how frequently people interact with their mobile devices, providing data on daily touches and usage patterns.

"Time Flies: U.S. Adults Now Spend Nearly Half a Day Interacting with Media," Nielsen, June 27, 2018, https://www.nielsen.com/insights/2018/time-flies-us-adults-now-spend-nearly-half-a-day-interacting-with-media/. Research showing Americans spend over 11 hours per day interacting with various forms of media, including TV, radio, smartphones, and digital platforms.

Gloria Mark, *Attention Span: A Groundbreaking Way to Restore Balance, Happiness and Productivity* (Hanover Square Press, 2023), 74. Research on modern attention span collapse to 47 seconds and the impact of technology on focus and cognitive function.

Gloria Mark, *Attention Span: A Groundbreaking Way to Restore Balance, Happiness and Productivity* (Hanover Square Press, 2023), 81. Foundational research showing that notifications can derail focus for up to 25 minutes, demonstrating the cognitive cost of technological interruptions.

"One third of your life is spent at work," Gettysburg College, accessed August, 2025, https://www.gettysburg.edu/news/stories?id=79db7b34-630c-4f49-ad32-4ab9ea48e72b. Analysis of lifetime work hours and career time investment, providing context for how Americans spend their productive years.

Brett Hautop, interview by author, Zoom, April 1, 2025. Former VP of Workplace at LinkedIn and Founding Partner at Workshape, discussing corporate workspace design, human connection to built environments, and the disconnect between designed spaces and human preferences.

Chapter 3: Muddy Boots Are Bad for Business

Phil Knight, *Shoe Dog: A Memoir by the Creator of Nike* (Scribner, 2016), 3. Memoir recounting Knight's early morning run revelation that he wanted his life to be play, the foundational idea that led to creating Nike, illustrating how movement can spark life-changing insights.

"About Cromford Mills," The Arkwright Society, accessed August, 2025, https://www.cromfordmills.org.uk/about/our-history/. Historical account of Richard Arkwright's first water-powered textile mill, opened in 1771, marking the beginning of the industrial revolution and the shift of work from outdoors to indoors.

"The Office As Facility Based on Change," Herman Miller, accessed August 2025, https://www.hermanmiller.com/products/workspaces/workstations/action-office-system/

design-story/. Documentation of Robert Propst's "Action Office II" system, launched in 1968, the first cubicle system designed to organize humans in office environments.

Walter Isaacson, *Steve Jobs* (Simon & Schuster, 2011), 324–325. Biography detailing Jobs's habit of conducting important business meetings while walking, including the pivotal barefoot walk with Microsoft's Greg Maffei that led to key software integration agreements shaping Apple's future.

Yvon Chouinard, *Let My People Go Surfing: The Education of a Reluctant Businessman (*Penguin Books, 2005), 61. Source describing how Chouinard took his top managers on a walkabout in Argentina during Patagonia's financial crisis, demonstrating how walking and movement can facilitate breakthrough thinking and organizational transformation.

Boris Veldhuijzen van Zanten, "Inspiring Entrepreneurs: What Netflix CEO Reed Hastings Has Learned in His Business Career," The Next Web, September 12, 2013, https://thenextweb.com/news/inspiring-entrepreneurs-reed-hastings-netflix. Reed Hastings's own account of the $40 late-fee incident for Apollo 13 as the defining moment that sparked the idea for Netflix.

Mitch Waldrop, "Einstein's Relativity Explained in 4 Simple Steps," National Geographic, May 16, 2017, https://www.nationalgeographic.com/science/article/einstein-relativity-thought-experiment-train-lightning-genius. Account of Einstein's breakthrough moment in May 1905 while walking to work with his best friend Michele Besso in Bern, where after discussing his relativity dilemma, Einstein worked through the solution overnight and told Besso the next morning, "Thank you. I've completely solved the problem."

Nikola Tesla, *My Inventions: The Autobiography of Nikola Tesla*. (Originally published in 1919, compiled by Ben Johnston, 1983), 22. Tesla's own account of his February 1882 epiphany in Budapest's City Park while walking with friend and reciting Goethe's Faust, when the idea for alternating current "came like a flash of lightning and in an instant the truth was revealed."

Ruth Ann. Atchley, David L. Strayer, and Paul Atchley, "Creativity in the Wild: Improving Creative Reasoning through Immersion in Natural Settings," National Library of Medicine, December 12, 2012, https://pmc.ncbi.nlm.nih.gov/articles/PMC3520840/. University of Utah study by Dr. David Strayer and colleagues showing that four days of immersion in nature increased performance on creativity and problem-solving tasks by 50 percent, supporting the cognitive benefits of sustained nature exposure.

Chapter 4: Hike or Walk

Francine Shapiro, *Eye Movement Desensitization and Reprocessing: Basic Principles, Protocols, and Procedures* (Guilford Press, 2001). Foundational text by the creator of EMDR therapy, documenting the discovery of bilateral stimulation effects during a walk in the park in 1987 and the development of therapeutic applications.

Gina Nelson, interview by author, Boise, May 4, 2025. Certified EMDR therapist and owner of Authentic Gains, explaining bilateral stimulation, the adaptive information processing model, and how walking creates therapeutic benefits similar to EMDR therapy.

Friedrich Nietzsche, *Twilight of the Idols; or, How to Philosophize with the Hammer*, trans. Anthony M. Ludovici (T. N. Foulis, 1911), 6. Classic aphorism: "Only those thoughts that come by walking have any value," reflecting the philosophical link between movement and creative thinking.

Walter Isaacson, *Steve Jobs* (Simon & Schuster, 2011.) Biography detailing Jobs's habit of conducting important business meetings while walking.

Jonny Evans, "Here is why Apple's Steve Jobs loved to walk and so should you," Apple Must, last modified April 6, 2025, https://www.applemust.com/here-is-why-apples-steve-jobs-loved-to-walk-and-so-should-you/. Jony Ive remembers walking around a flower garden with Steve Jobs to agree upon the final design of the iMac G4.

Dan Mitchell, "Silicon Valley's different kind of power walk," Fortune, last modified November 11th, 2011, https://fortune.com/2011/11/15/silicon-valleys-different-kind-of-power-walk/. Highlights the habits of Silicon Valley tech CEO's walking including Steve Jobs and Mark Zuckerberg being seen walking together in Palo Alto and Zuckerberg adopting the habit in his own life.

Adam Janofsky, "3 Time-Management Tips From Twitter and Square CEO Jack Dorsey," Inc. last modified October 16,2025, https://www.inc.com/adam-janofsky/how-jack-dorsey-is-surviving-the-most-mind-numbingly-busy-week-imaginable.html/. Dorsey talks about making time for planning and reflection including that "The best thinking time is just walking."

Loren Cordain, et al., "Achieving Hunter-Gatherer Fitness in the 21st Century: Back to the Future," The American

Journal of Medicine, December, 2010, https://www.amjmed.com/article/s0002-9343(10)00463-8/fulltext. Research on traditional movement patterns compared to modern sedentary lifestyles, supporting data on hunter-gatherer daily movement distances.

Herman Pontzer, et al., "Hunter-Gatherer Energetics and Human Obesity," National Library of Medicine, July 25, 2012, https://pubmed.ncbi.nlm.nih.gov/22848382/. Research comparing modern activity levels to traditional hunter-gatherer movement patterns, showing the dramatic decrease in daily movement from 8 to 15 miles to under 1.5 miles.

Christopher W. Lee, and Pim Cuijpers, "A Meta-Analysis of the Contribution of Eye Movements in Processing Emotional Memories," Journal of Behavior Therapy and Experimental Psychiatry, https://www.sciencedirect.com/science/article/abs/pii/S0005791612001000. Meta-analysis supporting the scientific basis of bilateral stimulation and eye movement in emotional processing, providing evidence for EMDR effectiveness.

Marily Oppezzo, Daniel L. Schwartz, "Give Your Ideas Some Legs: The Positive Effect of Walking on Creative Thinking," National Library of Medicine, April 21, 2014, https://pubmed.ncbi.nlm.nih.gov/24749966/. Stanford research demonstrating that walking, especially outdoors, can boost creative thinking by up to 60 percent, with benefits persisting after the walk ends. Walking outside produced the most novel and highest quality analogies.

Bethany Agusala, "Focusing on 10,000 Steps a Day Could Be a Misstep," UT Southwestern Medical Center, August 1, 2025, https://utswmed.org/medblog/how-many-steps-per-day/. Analysis of daily step counts and movement patterns, providing context for modern sedentary lifestyle compared to historical movement patterns.

John Finch, interview by author, Zoom, May 9, 2025. CEO and president of The Legacy Group, discussing the decision to incorporate hiking into the company keynote presentation and subsequent organizational changes including walking meetings.

Rick Rice, interview by author, Phone, May 9, 2025. Sales and project manager of The Legacy Group, discussing the impact of the Hike to Become Experience on his personal life.

Chapter 5: In Nature: We Trust

Hugh Asher, "The Origins of Forest Bathing," SilvoTherapy, June 18, 2024, https://silvotherapy.co.uk/articles/the-origins-of-forest-bathing. Historical context of forest bathing development in Japan, documenting the connection between karōshi (death by overwork) health crisis in the 1970s and 1980s, and the government's 1982 introduction of shinrin-yoku as a therapeutic response to urbanization and overwork.

Bum Jin Park, et al., "The Physiological Effects of Shinrin-Yoku (Taking in the Forest Atmosphere or Forest Bathing): Evidence from Field Experiments in 24 Forests Across Japan," SpringerNature Link, May 2, 2010, https://doi.org/10.1007/s12199-009-0086-9. Comprehensive Japanese study comparing forest versus city environments, showing specific physiological benefits including 13.4 percent cortisol reduction from viewing trees and 15.8 percent reduction from walking through forests, plus improvements in pulse rate and blood pressure.

Christian Arzberger, *Forest Bathing Incl. Nature Therapy and Silence*. Online education course, Treeming.org, 2023. accessed August, 2025. Guide to forest bathing practices including information about terpenes and fungal spores that trees emit to communicate, and their health benefits when inhaled by humans during nature immersion.

Genevive R. Meredith, et al., "Minimum Time Dose in Nature to Positively Impact Mental Health of College-Aged Students, and How to Measure It: A Scoping Review," Frontiers in Psychology, January 13, 2020, https://doi.org/10.3389/fpsyg.2019.02942. Review of over 14 studies showing that just 10 minutes or more spent sitting or walking in natural settings can significantly improve psychological and physiological biomarkers of mental well-being.

MaryCarol R. Hunter, Brenda W. Gillespie, and Sophie Yu-Pu Chen, "Urban Nature Experiences Reduce Stress in the Context of Daily Life Based on Salivary Biomarkers," Frontiers in Psychology, April 03, 2019. https://doi.org/10.3389/fpsyg.2019.00722. University of Michigan study by Dr. MaryCarol Hunter establishing the minimum effective dose of nature exposure for stress reduction, showing optimal cortisol reduction occurs with 20-30 minutes of nature experience.

Brett Hautop, interview by author, Zoom, April 1, 2025. Former VP of Workplace at LinkedIn and founder of Workshape, discussing controlled experiments comparing identical work settings indoors versus outdoors and consistent preference for outdoor environments.

Amy S. McDonnell, and David L. Strayer, "Immersion in Nature Enhances Neural Indices of Executive Attention," Scientific Reports, January 22, 2024, https://doi.org/10.1038/s41598-024-52205-1. University of Utah research demonstrating that walking in nature shows increased cognitive function and executive control than walking in urban environments.

Dr. Zane Sterling, interview by author, Boise, April 15, 2025. Client and serial entrepreneur discussing the experience of strategic planning sessions conducted on hiking trails versus traditional office settings, and the enhanced creativity and clarity achieved through nature-based business consultation.

Phil Knight, *Shoe Dog: A Memoir by the Creator of Nike* (Scribner, 2016), 3. Memoir describing the 1962 morning run in Portland, Oregon, that inspired the creation of Nike, illustrating how movement in nature can spark breakthrough business ideas.

Chapter 6: Keep Tech Off

Charles Darwin, *On the Origin of Species by Means of Natural Selection.* (John Murray, 1859). Darwin's foundational work developing his theory of evolution by natural selection, based largely on observations made during his voyage on HMS Beagle, particularly his time walking and observing wildlife in the Galápagos Islands.

Francine Shapiro, *Eye Movement Desensitization and Reprocessing: Basic Principles, Protocols, and Procedures* (Guilford Press, 2001). Foundational text by the creator of EMDR therapy, documenting the discovery of bilateral stimulation effects during a walk in the park in 1987 and the development of therapeutic applications.

Phil Knight, *Shoe Dog: A Memoir by the Creator of Nike* (Scribner, 2016), 3. Memoir describing the 1962 morning run in Portland, Oregon, that inspired the creation of Nike, illustrating how movement in nature can spark breakthrough business ideas.

Grayson Sterling, interview by author, Boise, April 15, 2025. Mental performance coach and former college athlete discussing the psychological dependency on fitness tracking technology and the experience of disconnecting from smartwatch monitoring during nature immersion.

Gloria Mark, *Attention Span: A Groundbreaking Way to Restore Balance, Happiness and Productivity* (Hanover Square Press, 2023), 74. Research on modern attention span collapse to 47 seconds and the impact of technology on focus and cognitive function.

Gloria Mark, *Attention Span: A Groundbreaking Way to Restore Balance, Happiness and Productivity* (Hanover Square Press, 2023) 81. Foundational research showing that notifications can derail focus for up to 25 minutes, demonstrating the cognitive cost of technological interruptions.

Walter Isaacson, *Steve Jobs* (Simon & Schuster, 2011.) Biography detailing Jobs's habit of conducting important business meetings while walking.

Brett Hautop, interview by author, Zoom, April 1, 2025. Former VP of Workplace at LinkedIn and founder of Workshape, discussing workplace experiments removing devices and observing participant reactions, including panic responses to technology disconnection.

Chapter 7: Every Day: For 31 Days

James Clear, *Atomic Habits: Tiny Changes, Remarkable Results* (Avery, 2018). Research on habit formation showing it takes at least 18 days to form simple habits and 21 to 30 days for complex behavioral changes, providing scientific foundation for the 31-day challenge duration.

John Finch, interview by author, Zoom, May 9, 2025. CEO of The Legacy Group, discussing workplace culture transformation after implementing team hiking experiences and the Hike to Become Challenge, including changes in communication patterns and employee vulnerability in outdoor settings.

Phil Knight, *Shoe Dog: A Memoir by the Creator of Nike* (Scribner, 2016), 20. Memoir recounting the pivotal moment in Hawaii when Knight considered abandoning his entrepreneurial dreams before hearing the "*faint inner voice*" that guided him to continue, illustrating the role of solitude and reflection in major life decisions.

Chapter 8: Your Brain on Nature

Bryant Richardson, interview by author, Zoom, May 30, 2025. Founder and president of Real Blue Sky and Hike to Become Challenge participant, discussing the psychological processing benefits of solo nature immersion and accessing previously unrecognized emotions through the practice.

Ruth Ann Atchley, David L. Strayer, and Paul Atchley, "Creativity in the Wild: Improving Creative Reasoning through Immersion in Natural Settings," Plos One, December 12, 2012, https://doi.org/10.1371/journal.pone.0051474. Pivotal study showing 50 percent increase in creativity after four days of wilderness backpacking without electronic devices, comparing Remote Associates Test scores before and after nature immersion with Outward Bound participants.

David Strayer, interview by author, Zoom, May 13, 2025. Head of Cognition and Neuroscience at University of Utah, explaining the four attention networks (orienting, alerting, executive, and default mode), how modern technology hijacks these systems, and the neurological mechanisms behind nature's cognitive restoration effects.

Ethan Hood, "Instruments of the U: Applied Cognition Lab," University of Utah, June 25, 2025, https://attheu.utah.edu/health-medicine/instruments-of-the-u-applied-cognition-lab/. University article detailing Dr. David Strayer's current EEG research on nature's brain benefits, confirming that time outdoors without technology significantly improves cognitive function while phone use negates these restorative effects.

Courtney E Ackerman, "What is Kaplan's Attention Restoration Theory (ART)?," Positive Psychology, November 13, 2018, https://positivepsychology.com/attention-restoration-theory/. Attention Restoration Theory suggests nature helps restores our mental focus & reduce cognitive fatigue.

Rachel Kaplan, and Stephen Kaplan, *The Experience of Nature: A Psychological Perspective* (Cambridge University Press, 1989). Foundational research on Attention Restoration Theory, establishing the concepts of "soft fascination" versus "hard fascination" and how natural environments provide cognitive restoration through gentle engagement rather than forced attention.

David Strayer, "Restore Your Brain with Nature," TED, December 12, 2017, https://www.ted.com/talks/david_strayer_restore_your_brain_with_nature. TEDx presentation detailing controlled studies comparing brain patterns of participants walking in arboretums with and without phone use, demonstrating inattentional blindness and cognitive restoration through technology-free nature exposure.

Dakota Barney, and Jen Barney, personal interview, Zoom, March 31, 2025. Participants at Conscious Investor Growth Summit discussing breakthrough business idea development during guided nature hike and the cognitive shift from suppressed to accessible creative thinking in natural settings.

Christian Toebe, interview by author, Zoom, April 27, 2025. COO of Bovino Law Associates and regenerative farm owner, discussing how 75 percent of business innovations occur during unplugged outdoor activities and the neurological effects of cross-lateral movement on accessing creative problem-solving states.

Chapter 9: Becoming Fearless

Timothy D. Wilson, et al., "Just Think: The Challenges of the Disengaged Mind," Science, July 4, 2014, https://doi.org/10.1126/science.1250830. Landmark University of Virginia study involving 11 experiments with hundreds of participants, showing that 67 percent of men and 25 percent of women chose to self-administer electric shocks rather than sit alone with their thoughts for 6 to 15 minutes, demonstrating modern aversion to solitude and introspection.

Tracy Lube, interview by author, Zoom, May 9, 2025. Corporate sales operations and marketing executive turned consultant, discussing workplace fear, boundary-setting, and confidence transformation following the challenging Sedona desert hike experience and founding of HerMeno[SM] employee benefit service.

Out There: A National Parks Story, directed by Brenden Hall (Prom Creative, 2023), 00:44:45. https://www.outthere.film/. Documentary featuring stories of people who live, work, and travel through national parks, including backpacker Julia

Michalski's perspective on solo hiking and the quote "Fear just shouldn't inhibit you from doing beautiful things."

Chapter 10: Developing Radical Self-Awareness

Yancy Wright, interview by author, Zoom, April 18, 2025. CEO and founder of Casa Alternavida wellness retreat, former sustainability director at Sellen Construction, discussing his burnout experience leading to ICU hospitalization, transformational nature-based healing during kitesurfing trip to Venezuela, and somatic principles connecting emotional trauma to physical ailments, particularly the concept that back pain represents carrying others' burdens.

Michael A. Singer, *The Untethered Soul: The Journey Beyond Yourself*. (New Harbinger Publications, 2007). Spiritual and philosophical text on consciousness and inner freedom, brought along for reading during the technology-free backpacking experience at Havasu Falls as the only book packed for the five-day journey.

Chapter 11: Cultivating Powerful Presence

Tom Roberts, interview by author, Zoom, May 2, 2025. Former corporate executive turned consultant and founder of Cranberry Leadership, discussing corporate burnout experience, including clinical depression and blood pressure issues at career pinnacle, transformation through early morning conference hike, and successful implementation of Hike to Become Challenge while working in Japan.

Kimberly Moran, interview by author, Zoom, March 3, 2025. Executive leader at major medical company with PhD and

MBA, describing the Wahclella Falls team experience, forest bathing exercise impacts, personal discoveries during the Hike to Become Challenge, including improved listening and focus abilities, and ROI calculations for nature-based leadership development showing potential hundred-fold returns.

John Finch, interview by author, Zoom, May 9, 2025. CEO and president of Legacy Group, discussing how team hiking experiences facilitated deeper, more challenging conversations, increased team connection, and bravery in addressing difficult partnership topics.

Chapter 12: The Wild Advantage

Howard Schultz, and Dori Jones Yang. *Pour Your Heart Into It: How Starbucks Built a Company One Cup at a Time* (Hyperion, 1997). Memoir detailing how Schultz transformed Starbucks from a single coffee bean store into a global "third place" community gathering space, inspired by Italian coffee bar culture and Ray Oldenberg's sociological concept, proving that unconventional retail philosophy could redefine an entire industry.

Ray Oldenburg, *The Great Good Place: Cafes, Coffee Shops, Bookstores, Bars, Hair Salons, and Other Hangouts at the Heart of a Community* (Marlowe & Company, 1999), 14. Sociological work developing the "third place" concept that Howard Schultz used to transform Starbucks from coffee shops into community gathering spaces.

Ray C. Anderson, *Confessions of a Radical Industrialist: Profits, People, Purpose: Doing Business by Respecting the Earth.* (St. Martin's Press, 2009). Memoir documenting Interface Inc.'s transformation from petroleum-intensive carpet manufacturer to sustainable business model through "Mission Zero" initiative, proving that environmental responsibility and profitability can coexist.

"Don't Buy This Jacket," Patagonia, November 25, 2011, https://eu.patagonia.com/gb/en/stories/dont-buy-this-jacket-black-friday-and-the-new-york-times/story-18615.html. Full-page Black Friday advertisement urging consumers to reconsider purchases and highlighting environmental impact of consumption, resulting in 30 percent sales increase while promoting conscious consumption and the Common Threads Initiative.

Phil Knight, *Shoe Dog: A Memoir by the Creator of Nike* (Scribner, 2016), 3. Memoir containing the 1962 quote "...*I wanted my life to be. Play*" representing the foundational vision that led to Nike's creation.

Walter Isaacson, *Steve Jobs* (Simon & Schuster, 2011.) Biography detailing Jobs's habit of conducting important business meetings while walking.

Yvon Chouinard, *Let My People Go Surfing: The Education of a Reluctant Businessman* (Penguin Books, 2005), 162. Memoir and business philosophy book containing the foundational quote "*Let my people go surfing*" representing unconventional leadership and work-life integration principles.

John Bova, "Once a Month This CEO Kicks Staffers Out of the Office. Here's Why," Entrepreneur, January 23, 2024, https://www.entrepreneur.com/growing-a-business/how-a-monthly-hiking-day-boosts-productivity-at-alltrails/468579. Article documenting AllTrails' Trail Days program and the ROI of monthly nature-based innovation time, including the quote about trading screen time for positivity and impact being a "no-brainer investment."

Ron Schneidermann, interview by author, Zoom, May 9, 2025. Former CEO of AllTrails discussing Trail Days innovation program, strategic planning in Yosemite, relationship between nature immersion and business innovation, and the 75 percent statistic for Trail Days-inspired innovations, including the Apple Watch app development.

Kimberly Moran, personal interview, Zoom, March 3, 2025. Executive leader discussing how nature-based experiences help people access internal answers rather than relying on expensive consultants, and transformation of team meeting formats and strategic initiatives.

Tom Roberts, interview by author, Zoom, May 5, 2025. Former corporate executive discussing the concept of *"creating space for magic to happen"* through proactive outdoor experiences vs. traditional work approaches.

John Finch, interview by author, Zoom, May 9, 2025. CEO of The Legacy Group, discussing belief in unconventional keynote format and early support for the Hike to Become approach.

About the Author

Jessica DeAngelo is the Chief Hiking Officer and founder of Hike to Become®, where she guides people to unlock their boldest ideas outside. A TEDx speaker and creator of the Hike to Become Challenge, she's worked with leaders from Fortune 500 companies like Amazon, Nike, and Uber. Hike to Become offers a science-backed, outdoor approach to solving business challenges and sparking innovative ideas. Jessica creates epic experiences, including keynotes, strategy sessions, and executive retreats that help impact-driven teams trade boardroom burnout for breakthrough clarity. She lives in Boise with her husband and two fierce little humans who remind her daily that the best adventures always start with good snacks.

Jessica can be reached at:
www.jessicadeangelo.com

www.ingramcontent.com/pod-product-compliance
Lightning Source LLC
Chambersburg PA
CBHW020538030426
42337CB00013B/895